EMPIRES OF ANCIENT PERSIA

GREAT EMPIRES OF THE PAST

EMPIRES OF ANCIENT PERSIA

MICHAEL BURGAN

THOMAS G. URBAN, HISTORICAL CONSULTANT

CHELSEA HOUSE PUBLISHERS

An imprint of Infobase Publishing

Great Empires of the Past: Empires of Ancient Persia

Chelsea House
An imprint of Infobase Publishing
132 West 31st Street
New York NY 10001

Library of Congress Cataloging-in-Publication Data
Burgan, Michael.
  Empires of ancient Persia / Michael Burgan.
    p. cm.—(Great empires of the past)
  Includes bibliographical references and index.
  ISBN 978-1-60413-156-7
  1. Iran—Juvenile literature. 2. Iran—History—To 640—Juvenile literature. 3. Iran—Civilization—To 640—Juvenile literature.
I. Title. II. Series.

  DS254.75.B87 2009
  935—dc22

                              2009011154

Produced by the Shoreline Publishing Group LLC
Editorial Director: James Buckley Jr.
Series Editor: Beth Adelman
Text design by Annie O'Donnell
Cover design by Alicia Post
Composition by Mary Susan Ryan-Flynn
Cover printed by Bang Printing, Brainerd, MN
Book printed and bound by Bang Printing, Brainerd, MN
Date printed: November 2009
Printed in the United States of America

10 9 8 7 6 5 4 3 2 1

CONTENTS

INTRODUCTION

FOR ALMOST 1,200 YEARS, FROM 550 B.C.E. TO 651 C.E., THE Persians dominated an area that stretched from the Black Sea (which is north of modern Turkey and bordered by Eastern Europe) into Central Asia. Throughout its long history, Persia had contact with—and often battled—many of the other great empires of the past.

The Persian homeland was centered in the southwest of modern-day Iran, along the Zagros Mountains. From there, the Persians conquered the various kingdoms of Mesopotamia, in the region between the Tigris and Euphrates Rivers in what is now Iraq. They then spread their influence over Egypt and the fringes of southern Europe. This made them the first empire builders to control part of three continents. To the east, Persian rule extended as far as India.

It is difficult to talk about one Persian Empire, because three distinct Persian peoples rose to power at different times. But they shared a similar language and culture and ruled many of the same lands. The Achaemenid dynasty created what is sometimes called the Persian Empire. Their rule lasted from about 559 B.C.E. until 330 B.C.E., when Persia was conquered by Alexander the Great (356–323 B.C.E.). Several centuries later, the Parthians rose to power in the region. They were followed by the Sassanians.

For centuries, historians in Europe and North America studied the Persians mostly through the words of ancient Greek and Roman writers. Their writings provided important information on Persian history and culture. But the ancient Greeks and Romans saw the Persians as their enemies, and so their accounts of the Persians were not always accurate.

OPPOSITE
This golden chariot (a horse-drawn cart that carries soldiers) is a symbol of both the wealth and power of the Persian Empire.

CONNECTIONS

What Are Connections?

Throughout this book, and all the books in the Great Empires of the Past series, there are Connections boxes. They point out ideas, inventions, art, food, customs, and more from this empire that are still part of the world today. Nations and cultures in remote history can seem far away from the present day, but these connections demonstrate how our everyday lives have been shaped by the peoples of the past.

Starting in the 19th century, archaeologists (scientists who study ancient peoples by studying the items they left behind) began to translate ancient Persian writings. They also discovered new sources of information from lands that bordered Persia. Although the Persians did not write complete history books, government records helped present the Persians' view of their world. So did writings, called inscriptions, carved into great monuments and tombs of the empire's leaders.

From both Western and Persian sources, a picture emerges of an empire that allowed the local people in its distant regions to control much of their own affairs. The Persians borrowed ideas from the people they conquered and let them keep their local language and customs. In his book *The Histories*, Greek historian Herodotus (ca. 484–ca. 425 B.C.E.) wrote, "The Persians welcome foreign customs more than any other people."

The lands the Persians controlled provided a great deal of wealth. They used it to construct massive buildings and make great art. They introduced the Persian language and culture in large parts of Central Asia, and that influence remains today beyond the borders of Iran. And some Persian words and concepts also entered Western culture—connections to the present that will be explored throughout this book.

PEOPLE OF THE STEPPE

The Persians traced their roots to people who came out of the steppe, a vast, flat, and mostly treeless area that stretches across Central Asia into parts of Eastern Europe. The steppe people were great horsemen—horses were first ridden by humans who lived on the steppe of modern-day Ukraine more than 4,000 years ago.

The culture that developed in that part of the steppe eventually spread eastward across Asia. Then, by about 1000 B.C.E., some descen-

The clash between Persia and Greece was recorded by Greek historian Herodotus.

dants (relatives who trace their roots back to one person) of those steppe dwellers called the Medes and Persians settled in southwest Iran. They settled on a plateau (a high, flat area of land) near the Zagros Mountains and the Persian Gulf. This region is in an area known as the Near East—part of southwest Asia bordering the Mediterranean, Black, and Caspian Seas, and the Persian Gulf.

Some of the world's first great civilizations appeared in a part of the Near East called the Fertile Crescent. This was a crescent, or arc-shaped, area of land that began at the northern end of the Persian Gulf, ran through Mesopotamia, and curved southward toward what is now Israel. In the Fertile Crescent, farming first developed about 12,000 years ago.

When the Medes and Persians entered the Near East, the Fertile Crescent was divided up into several small kingdoms. In northern Mesopotamia, the Assyrians were the dominant military power. Over the next several centuries, Assyria expanded its empire. During this time, Media, the land of the Medes, grew stronger too. The two nations clashed in the seventh century, and Media joined with Babylonia to defeat the Assyrians.

Persia or Iran?

Most ancient Greek writers called the land of the Achaemenid dynasty *Persai*. This word came from what the Achaemenids themselves called the region—Parsua, or Persis. Today, this part of Iran is called Fars, and that is the root of the word *Farsi*, the modern Persian language spoken in Iran.

In English, *Persai* became "Persia," and Western writers have used that name to refer to the home of the ancient Persians and the lands they conquered. The ancient Persians, however, usually called their land *Eire-An* or *Ir-An*, meaning "Land of the Aryans." The first Persians were a people who called themselves Aryans, and came to southwest Asia from the northeast.

In 1935, the government of Persia officially changed the country's name to Iran. In this book, *Iran* refers to the modern country of that name and *Persia* refers to the ancient empire.

The Fertile Crescent Today

The Fertile Crescent has been called the "cradle of civilization," and descendants of some of the world's very first farmers still live in the region today. At the end of the 20th century, the people and the environment of the Fertile Crescent faced a growing threat. Satellite pictures showed that marshlands along the border of Iraq and Iran were disappearing. The affected areas could have completely dried up within a few years.

Building dams along the Tigris and Euphrates Rivers, along with draining the wetlands, has led to the problem. As the marshland disappeared, animals that lived in the region died, and the people were forced to leave to find water. Many became refugees—people forced to leave their homes because of natural disasters or war. About 500,000 of them settled in Iran.

Thanks to the United Nations, Iran and especially Iraq took steps to return water to the marshlands, ensuring they would not disappear.

Babylonia had once been the dominant power in Mesopotamia, hundreds of years before the Assyrians came to power. Now, for a time, the Babylonians controlled the region again. The Medes, however, had their own growing kingdom. They also had influence over some neighboring states, including Persis, the land of the Persians.

THE RISE OF THE PERSIANS

In the middle of the sixth century B.C.E., a Persian named Cyrus II (ca. 585–529 B.C.E.) became king in Anshan, the western part of Persis. Through his mother, he may have been related to Astyages (r. 584–550 B.C.E.), the king of Media. But historians are not sure. Cyrus II united all of Persis under his rule. This marked the beginning of the Achaemenid dynasty. He then angered Astyages by refusing to accept Medean influence over Persis.

Around 550 B.C.E., Astyages launched an attack on Cyrus and his troops. According to the *Babylonian Chronicles*, an ancient collection of government records, Astyages' men turned against their king, and Cyrus won a quick and decisive victory. Soon he ruled over Media, too. Other Persian tribes north of that kingdom also pledged their loyalty to Cyrus.

The new, united Persian-Median state was stronger than it had been when the two groups were separate. Drawing on this strength, Cyrus began a long career of conquest. He defeated Lydia, in what is now western Turkey, and then conquered Babylonia and neighboring lands to the west.

Cyrus also turned to the east and won battles across Central Asia, bringing the borders of his new empire to what is now Tajikistan. In 529 B.C.E., Cyrus died in battle. Future historians called him Cyrus the Great, in honor of his achievements. As modern historian Maria Brosius writes in *The Persians*, "Under the leadership of a single king, the Persians had become the dominant power of the known world."

Cambyses II (d. 522 B.C.E.), Cyrus's son, became the next king of the Persians. He continued to expand his father's empire. Cambyses won control of Egypt and Cyprus, an island in the Mediterranean Sea. When he died, a nobleman named Darius (ca. 550–486 B.C.E.) claimed the throne. So did a supposed brother of Cambyses named Bardiya (d. ca. 525 B.C.E.). Darius and his supporters defeated Bardiya, and Darius became ruler of the Persians.

Persian Names

The names used for Persian leaders in most history books actually come from Greek and Latin writers. *Cyrus*, for example is the Latin version of the Greek name *Kouros*, which came from the Old Persian name *Kurush*. Other well-known Persian names have gone through similar changes. *Darius,* the name of several important Persian kings, is the Latin version of the Greek name for the Old Persian *Darayavaush*. *Xerxes* is the Greek name for two leaders known in Old Persian as *Krshayarsha*. Throughout this book, the more common Latin and Greek versions of Persian names have been used.

Under Darius, the Persian Empire expanded even more. Darius pushed across Central Asia and into northwestern India. He also invaded Europe, entering Scythia, which was the home of another Aryan people. (Scythia was a region north of the Black Sea in modern-day Ukraine and Russia). This region did not come under Persian control, but Thrace and Macedonia did. (These lands were southwest of Scythia in what is now Macedonia, Greece, Bulgaria, and western Turkey.)

WARS AND DEFEAT

The Greek city-states in Lydia had become part of the empire in 546 B.C.E, and they rose in rebellion in 499 B.C.E. (City-states are independent political units consisting of a city and the surrounding countryside that comes under its rule.) Greek settlers had come to the region several hundred years before, and they wanted their independence from Persian rule. At the time, Greece was made up of independent city-states scattered across the Aegean Sea. Citizens of Athens and other city-states supported their fellow Greeks. Darius defeated the rebels, and then turned to attack Greece itself.

Greece and Persia already competed to control trade in the region. Now, the Persian invasion in 490 B.C.E. brought the two great powers into direct military conflict. The Greeks united to defeat the Persians twice over the next decade. But kings after Darius would continue to try to weaken Greek power.

During the fourth century B.C.E., Persia's rulers dealt with various regional rebellions. The empire was divided into regions called satrapies. Egypt was one satrapy that successfully won its independence for a time. The residents of other satrapies, including Phoenicia

 CONNECTIONS

Stan in Central Asia

Several of the countries of Central Asia have names that end in *stan*. Some examples are Afghanistan and Pakistan. This suffix has its roots in Persian and means "place of." So the name of the people who lived in a region was added to *stan* when the area was named. For example, Kazakhstan is the place where the Kazakh people live.

For a time, the Persians called what are now India and Pakistan *Hindustan*, meaning it was the place of the people who followed the Hindu religion.

The world map gained a number of new *stans* after the breakup of the Soviet Union in 1991. Many Central Asian peoples who had been part of the Soviet Republics gained their independence when the Soviet Union collapsed. These new nations include Tajikistan, Uzbekistan, and Turkmenistan.

(along the Mediterranean coast of the Fertile Crescent) also rebelled. Ending these rebellions cost the government money and soldiers.

The Achaemenids also had their own squabbles, and members of the royal family or their aides sometime battled each other for control. Darius III (d. 330 B.C.E.) came to power in 336 B.C.E., after some royal infighting. He turned out to be the last Achaemenid king.

IN THEIR OWN WORDS

The Father of History

The clash between Persia and Greece was first recorded in *The Histories* (sometimes called *The Persian Wars*) by Herodotus (ca. 484–ca. 425 B.C.E.). This Greek writer has been called the Father of History, because he was the first known historian. He traveled through many of the lands he described in his book.

To write *The Histories*, Herodotus used facts that he gathered on his own, plus stories he heard from people he met. To write about Persia, Herodotus recounts information dating back to the founding of the Persian Empire, not merely from the time of the war with Greece.

Some historians have criticized him for including myths (traditional stories, sometimes involving gods or magic), or not clearly separating the myths from the facts. Herodotus was also influenced by the general Greek idea that Persians were strange and uncivilized. This is a part of his description of their customs.

It is the Persian custom to regard a person's birthday as the most important day of the year for him. They consider it their duty to serve larger quantities at dinner on their birthday than they do on any other day. Well-off Persians serve an ox, a horse, a camel, or a donkey, roasted whole in an oven. Poor Persians serve some smaller creature from their flocks. They do not eat many main courses as a rule, but they eat a lot of extra courses, and not all together. . . .

They are extremely fond of wine, and they are not supposed to vomit or urinate when anyone else can see them. Although they have to be careful about all that, it is usual for them to be drunk when they are debating the most important issues. However, any decision they reach is put to them again on the next day, when they are sober, by the head of the household where the debate takes place. If they still approve of it when they are sober, it is adopted, but otherwise they forget about it. And any issues they debate when sober are reconsidered when they are drunk.

Herodotus's *The Histories* gives a colorful view of the ancient world, but one that must be balanced with modern research to get a true picture.

(Source: Herodotus. *The Histories*. Translated by Robin Waterfield. Oxford, U.K.: Oxford University Press, 1998.)

Satraps and Satrapies

A Persian satrapy was headed by a person called a satrap, a kind of governor. The two words came from the Old Persian word *xsacapavan* (or *khshatrapavan*), which means "defender of the kingdom." A satrap had a good deal of control over his province, but the land still came under the rule of the Persian king.

A Greek and Macedonian force led by Alexander the Great invaded Central Asia in 334 B.C.E. Within three years, Darius was dead and Alexander ruled the Persian Empire—though only briefly. Alexander died in 323 B.C.E., and Mesopotamia, Persia, and most of Central Asia came under the control of one of his generals, Seleucus (ca. 358–281 B.C.E.). Seleucus was the founder of the Seleucid dynasty, which ruled parts of the old Persian Empire for the next several hundred years.

PARTHIAN PERSIA

To the Persians, the Greeks were outsiders, not their true rulers. This included Seleucus. As a result, some regions began to break away from Seleucid rule. One of these was Parthia, a region east of Media and Persis along the Caspian Sea. The Parni, an Aryan tribe with roots in Central Asia, had come to the region around 300 B.C.E. By 247 B.C.E., a Parni named Arsaces (r. ca. 248–211 B.C.E.) ruled part of the satrapy, and he took full control within a decade. This marked the start of the Parthian Empire.

Over the next several decades, Arsaces and the rulers after him took more Seleucid lands, building a new Persian Empire. The Parthians traded with China to the east; Asian goods going to Europe went through their lands. The Parthians also came into conflict with the Roman Empire, which had become the dominant power in Europe. The two empires fought for control of Mesopotamia and neighboring lands.

The Parthian rulers saw themselves as carrying on the rule of the Achaemenids. They wanted to assert Parthia's power over traditional Persian lands. The Roman historian Tacitus (ca. 56–ca. 120 C.E.) wrote in *The Annals* that Parthian ruler Arabians II (d. ca. 40 C.E.) ". . . insisted on the ancient boundaries of Persia and Macedonia, and intimated [hinted] . . . that he meant to seize on the country [that had been] possessed by Cyrus and afterwards by Alexander."

The Roman Empire fought several fierce battles against the Parthians, from the 1st century B.C.E. into the 3rd century C.E. These wars were broken by short periods of peace, and then the fighting would begin again. Several times, the Romans captured the Parthian capital of Ctesiphon, but were then driven out. The rivalry between Persia and Rome would continue even after a new Persian dynasty forced the Parthians from power.

THE SASSANIAN EMPIRE AND COLLAPSE

A local king ruled Persis, although he pledged his loyalty to the Parthian king. Around 200 C.E., a member of a local noble family named Papak (d. ca. 212 C.E.) overthrew the local king. Papak then took control of the district of Istakhr, near Persepolis, the ruined ancient capital of Persis. Soon after he died, Papak's son Ardashir (d. 241 C.E.) made himself king of the district. He began to seize control of neighboring territory.

Parthian officials saw Ardashir gain more and more power, and they prepared to stop him. King Artabanus IV (d. 224 C.E.) led his army to Media in 224 C.E., where they battled Ardashir and his men. Ardashir killed the king and declared himself the new ruler of Parthia. His ruling family became known as the Sassanian dynasty, after the name of the man he claimed was his grandfather, Sassan.

Ardashir fought for several years to gain control of Parthia. Then his successors (the rulers who came after him) tried to retake lands that had been conquered centuries before by Cyrus and Darius. The Sassanians claimed a direct family link to the Achaemenid Persians of old, through Sassan. And, like the Parthians, the Sassanians fought several major wars with the Roman Empire in Mesopotamia, Armenia, and along the Mediterranean coast.

The struggle between the Romans and the Persians went on for several hundred years. It continued even after the western half of the Roman Empire split from the eastern half in 395 C.E. At times, the Sassanians also battled other neighboring peoples, such as the Arabs, Hephthalites, and Turks.

But the Persians of the Sassanian Empire were not just fighters. Their kings promoted the arts and education. They made Zoroastrianism the official religion of the empire, helping to spread its influence in the Near East and Central Asia. This religion had its roots in Persia and had been practiced by both Achaemenids and Parthians. But Zoroastrian priests now had more influence than ever before.

By the early 600s, the Sassanians were taking lands from the Romans along the Aegean and Mediterranean Seas—lands the ancient Persians had also conquered. But by the middle of the seventh century, the Sassanian Empire was crushed by a new power—the Arabs of Saudi Arabia. These Arabs built their own empire that stretched from North Africa to Central Asia, and included southern Spain.

The Sassanian Dynasty

Persian and Arab sources are not clear about the ties between Sassan and Ardashir, although most say Sassan was Ardashir's grandfather. Not much is known about Sassan. He seems to have been the chief priest at a temple dedicated to the Persian prophet Zoroaster. One Persian source said he had family ties to the Achaemenid royal family. Most likely, this claim was made to tie Ardashir to that great Persian dynasty.

In modern times, one historian has suggested that Sassan could have been the name of another god worshipped in the ancient Near East. Whatever the truth about Sassan and his roots, his name lives on in the name of one of the great empires of the ancient world.

The Roman Empire fought with the Parthians several times. This Roman monument was built after the end of the Parthian wars to honor the victories of Emperor Lucius Verus, who commanded the Roman forces.

In the former Sassanian lands, the Persian influence remained strong. Persians also traveled throughout the new Islamic Empire, working for the Arabs. Others became refugees who fled to India and Byzantium (the eastern half of the old Roman Empire).

Today, Iran (and, to some extent, Iraq) holds some of the great examples of Persian art and architecture. Even beyond the ancient borders of the empire, Persian influence thrives. The ancient Persian religion, Zoroastrianism, is still followed today. The Persians helped make chess popular across Asia and Europe. And English speakers use words with their Persian roots, such as *bazaar*, *orange*, and *lemon*. The history of the three Persian Empires is the history of a people who still have an impact on today's world.

PART·I

HISTORY

THE FIRST PERSIAN EMPIRE

THE ACHAEMENID EMPIRE AT ITS LARGEST

THE NEW PERSIAN EMPIRES

CHAPTER 1

THE FIRST PERSIAN EMPIRE

THE AGRICULTURAL LIFE THAT DEVELOPED IN THE FERTILE Crescent brought great changes to human society. The peoples of southwest Asia began to produce enough food to support larger populations. The food included products from domesticated animals, such as cattle, goats, and sheep. Within societies, some people developed specific roles as priests, leaders, or artisans (specialists in a particular craft).

A number of early city-states developed in Mesopotamia, along the Tigris and Euphrates Rivers and farther east toward the Zagros Mountains. Sumer was one of the most important. The Sumerians built huge temples, traded with other regions, and developed the first writing system, called cuneiform.

Around 2250 B.C.E., the Akkadians became a major force in Mesopotamia. They created what has been called the region's first empire. It is thought that the Akkadians originally formed a part of the Sumerian civilization; however, they spoke a Semitic language that differed from Sumerian. By defeating the Sumerians, neighboring people called the Elamites, and other city-states, the Akkadians controlled a band of land that stretched from the Persian Gulf to the Mediterranean Sea. Their capital, Akkad, was just south of modern-day Baghdad.

When their empire fell, around 2125 B.C.E., independent city-states appeared again. One of them, Ur, managed to extend its control beyond the Zagros Mountains.

Around 2000 B.C.E., the Babylonians emerged as a power and built a kingdom in the region. Babylon competed with Assyria for influence in Mesopotamia, and by about 1000 B.C.E. Assyria was the region's

OPPOSITE
Aristocrats of the Achaemenid court are shown in this relief carving, which once decorated a palace staircase.

main power. Around that time, a new people began to appear on the fringes of the Fertile Crescent—the Aryans.

THE MEDES AND THE PERSIANS

The Aryans first arose north and east of the Caspian Sea, in what is now western Kazakhstan. In their language, the root of their name means "noble." The Aryans traced their origins to earlier people known today as the Proto-Indo-Europeans. They first appeared either in Anatolia (most of modern Turkey, also called Asia Minor), or a region bordering southern Ukraine and Russia. From these Indo-Europeans came a group of languages that includes Persian, English, and most European languages.

The Aryans spread out across the steppe of Central Asia. Some headed north into Russia and others reached India. The Aryans relied on horses for transportation and in warfare. They, or people related to them, built the first battle chariots (horse-drawn carts that carry soldiers). The Aryans, with their horses and other grazing animals, were nomads—people who move from place to place with no permanent home.

Some Aryans reached southwest Asia around 1500 B.C.E. and settled in what is now Syria, Turkey, and Iraq. They blended in with the local people. The second wave of Aryans came around 1000 B.C.E. and included the Medes and the Persians. Their language and culture slowly spread in the region of the Zagros Mountains, replacing the native culture.

The Medes settled in what is now northwest Iran. The city of Ecbatana (modern Hamadan) was in the center of the Median homeland. The Persians founded Persis in southwest Iran, close to the Persian Gulf.

Both tribes came into contact with various peoples who already lived on and around the Iranian Plateau. The most important, especially for the Persians, were the Elamites. Their kingdom of Elam was centuries old, and the Elamites had their own cuneiform for their language. Their cities included Susa and Anshan. These remained important urban centers under later Persian rule.

In the years after the arrival of the Medes and Persians, the Assyrians extended their direct control over more of the Near East. Their empire grew to include Syria and Babylonia—the city of Babylon and the lands around it. The Assyrians were the first to write about the

Medes, during the ninth century B.C.E.

Writing about 400 years later, Greek historian Herodotus explained what he knew about the rise of Media as a kingdom. In *The Histories*, he tells of Deioces (r. 699–647 B.C.E.), a judge who won the respect of his fellow citizens. To bring order to the Medes, the people decided to choose a king. Herodotus wrote, "Deioces was so much in everyone's mouth [spoken about], that all ended by agreeing that he should be their king."

Persian and Median soldiers are shown here, symbolizing the two peoples who together formed the Persian Empire.

Modern historians do not know if Herodotus's report is true. If it is, the Medes might have united to resist Assyrian attacks. Starting in the ninth century B.C.E., the Assyrians conducted raids into both Media and Persis. For a time, the Assyrians controlled land east of Media and founded a city they called Tah-a-Ran. (Today that city is Tehran, the capital of Iran.) The Assyrians also battled Medes who fought on foot in the mountains.

The Assyrians forced the Medes to pay tribute (money or goods paid to a foreign ruler to prevent an invasion or show obedience). This included horses, sheep, and camels. And, in a common Assyrian practice, a group of Medes were sent out of their homeland in the seventh century B.C.E. and forced to live in Assyria. The Medes had to work for the Assyrians and had no contact with their homeland.

RISE OF A NEW NATION

In the first decades of the seventh century, nomads from the north called Scythians (sometimes written as *Saka*) and Cimmerians attacked Assyria and Media. The Scythians were the stronger of the two groups, and for a time, they controlled Media.

CONNECTIONS

Kurdish Fighters

The descendants of the Medes in northern Iran include the Kurds. Today they are spread out over a region that includes parts of Iraq, Iran, and Turkey, and smaller parts of Syria and Armenia—all of which was once part of the Persian Empire. Many Kurds want to create their own nation, and fighters known as *peshmerga* have often carried out this war for independence.

In the Iraq War, the *peshmerga* helped U.S. troops battle forces loyal to the government of Saddam Hussein. The name of these fighters means "those who face death." In his book *Shadows in the Desert*, historian Kaveh Farrokh suggests that the ancient Medes who fought in the mountains of Kurdistan against the Assyrians were the ancestors of the *peshmerga* in spirit and purpose.

The Medes, however, still kept their own king—Cyaxares (d. ca. 585 B.C.E.), the grandson of Deioces. The Scythians and Medes spoke a similar language, and the Medes had the Scythians teach their boys how to shoot a bow and arrow. Relations between the Scythians and Medes improved so much that they fought as allies against Assyria.

The Babylonians rebelled against Assyrian rule in 626 B.C.E. Ten years later, the Babylonians had secured control of their homeland and then invaded Assyria. Medes then joined the war. They invaded the Assyrian city of Ashur (Ash Sharqat in modern-day Iraq), and the Scythians soon fought along side them. In 612 B.C.E., the allies took over the Assyrian capital of Nineveh. Some accounts say the invaders directed the waters of a nearby river toward Nineveh, and this rushing force of nature helped take down the city's outer walls and gate. According to the *Babylonian Chronicles*, the Medes and their allies "carried off the vast booty [wealth] of the city and the temple and turned the city into a ruin heap."

In ancient Persis, the first soldiers were farmers who stepped up to fight when their tribe or kingdom faced attack. As an army, these soldiers were called *kara*. In Media, Cyaxares created a full-time army, called a *spada*. He likely imitated some of the organization of the Assyrian army, while also drawing on the strengths of the Medes as skilled horsemen. Herodotus wrote in *The Histories* that Cyaxares was the first Median ruler to separate the army into units of "spear-bearers, archers, and cavalry. Before this they were all mixed up . . . together." (Archers fight with a bow and arrow and cavalry soldiers fight on horseback.)

With the end of the Assyrian Empire, Babylonia and Media divided up its lands. Media received the old Assyrian homeland, centered in present-day Iraq, and nearby territory. In the decades that followed, Cyaxares expanded his kingdom to the north, into the Caucasus Mountains between the Caspian and Black Seas.

The Medes also turned to the west, pushing into Anatolia, where the kingdom of Lydia was the dominant power. A peace treaty of 585 B.C.E. ended the war, giving Cyaxares control of eastern Anatolia. To seal the peace, he arranged a marriage between his son Astyages (r. ca. 584–550 B.C.E.) and the daughter of the Lydian king.

Astyages became king of Media the next year, and he turned his armies toward the east. The Medes invaded the lands of Persian-speaking people in what is now eastern Iran. Then they continued into what is now Afghanistan. Even if the Medes did not directly control the lands they invaded, they at least influenced the local rulers. One of these partially independent states the Medes influenced was Persis.

THE BIRTH OF THE PERSIAN EMPIRE

While the Medes were creating an empire, the Persians were gaining influence in their region. After the destruction of the Elamite capital of Susa in the 640s B.C.E., Persis's neighbor Elam came under Assyrian control. Farther west was a second Elamite capital called Anshan. The city and surrounding region was soon ruled by a Persian dynasty founded by Teispes (r. ca. 635–610 B.C.E.). Teispes was the son of Achaemenes (dates unknown), whose name served as the dynastic name— the Achaemenids.

Teispes's grandson, Cambyses I (r. ca. 585–559 B.C.E.), later agreed to an alliance with Media. But the Medes were clearly the stronger of the two groups.

Some time around 575 B.C.E., Cambyses had a son, Cyrus. According to a few ancient sources, Cyrus's mother was the daughter of Astyages of Media. This establishes a family link between the two Persian kingdoms of Persis and Media. Some modern historians, however, doubt this claim is true.

Several ancient historians offered different stories about Cyrus's birth and childhood. In one version, his grandfather Astyages had a dream that suggested a grandson of his would become king. To prevent this, Astyages ordered that the newborn Cyrus be killed. But the Median official given the job could not bring himself to kill the baby, and instead gave him to a poor shepherd to raise.

In another story, Cyrus was actually the son of poor farmers. But he managed to find work with the Median rulers and became a favorite because of his great skill. Some modern historians point out that similar tales had been told about Near Eastern rulers before Cyrus. Ancient historians most likely took the basic structure of those earlier legends and adapted them for Cyrus, without any knowledge of the true facts of his early life.

Historians know that Cyrus took the throne in Anshan when he was still a teenager, in 559 B.C.E. He soon began one of the greatest series of conquests in world history.

By this time, Persis was actually divided into two smaller kingdoms. Cyrus began his military feats by uniting all of Persis under his rule.

Then, some time around 550 B.C.E., he went to war with Media. Details of the cause of the war are not clear. Astyages might have struck first, seeking to prevent Cyrus from becoming more powerful. Or Cyrus might have wanted to gain control of the Median king's territory.

In any event, some of the Median forces left Astyages to fight for Persis. They handed their king over to Cyrus. According to the *Babylonian Chronicles*, Cyrus then entered the Median capital of Ecbatana

CONNECTIONS

Remains of an Ancient Capital

To build his new capital of Pasargadae, Cyrus relied on skilled workers from Lydia and other neighboring lands. The results of their hard work are mostly gone today. Only the remains of a few buildings still stand in what was once a great city.

In the early 1960s, archaeologists starting digging at the site in southern Iran. They uncovered stone monuments, pottery, and jewels. In 2004, the United Nations Educational, Scientific, and Cultural Organization (UNESCO) named Pasargadae a World Heritage Site. This means the ruins of the ancient

Persian city are a unique part of world history and culture.

The ruins, however, now face possible damage. Ignoring the pleas of some archaeologists, in 2007 the government of Iran built a dam across a nearby river. The resulting reservoir threatened to wipe out an ancient road that once linked Pasargadae with the second Persian capital of Susa. The water could also destroy other ancient sites nearby. Some archaeologists fear that increased moisture in the air because of the dam could also harm Pasargadae, though others believe this is not a threat.

and "seized silver, gold, other valuables of the country . . . and brought [them] to Anshan."

Cyrus was now the king of a united Persia, and he built a new capital city called Pasargadae. Other Persian-speaking tribes of the region also accepted Cyrus as their king, and he was sometimes called the Great King. To modern historians, he is known as Cyrus the Great, the founder of the first Persian Empire.

After Cyrus united Media with the two kingdoms of Persis, he replaced the *kara* he had used with a professional army. This force grew in size as the now-united Persians con-

CONNECTIONS

As Rich as Croesus

The name of the ancient king of Lydia sometimes appears in modern conversations. If someone calls a person "as rich as Croesus," that person is very rich indeed, because Croesus was believed to be one of the wealthiest rulers of the Near East. Greeks who visited his capital of Sardis returned with tales of his wealth and the silver coins he minted.

Croesus is also remembered for asking the god Apollo whether he would defeat the Persians if he attacked them. The priest speaking for the god replied that Croesus "would destroy a mighty empire" (as Herodotus wrote in *The Histories*). Croesus assumed this meant he would beat the Persians. Instead, Cyrus won, and the great empire destroyed was Croesus's. The story is still told today to suggest the dangers of being too sure of oneself.

quered new lands and added new soldiers from those lands. Cyrus next looked northward and captured Urartu, a kingdom located near Lake Van, in what is now Turkey.

By around 547 B.C.E., the Persians' growing power worried Croesus (d. 546 B.C.E.), the king of Lydia. Croesus took an army across the border between his nation and Media. The Lydian forces included Greeks who lived in Lydia along the Aegean Sea. Croesus's and Cyrus's armies clashed near Cappadocia, in today's central Turkey.

Neither side won a clear victory, and Croesus pulled his troops back to Sardis, his capital in western Turkey. The Lydian king also sent some of his troops home for the winter. This proved to be a deadly mistake. Rather than pull back after the fighting at Cappadocia, Cyrus followed his enemy westward.

Croesus saw Cyrus getting ready for an attack, and quickly called for help from his allies, Egypt and Babylonia. But they could not respond in time. As part of his force, Cyrus had soldiers on camels who led the attack. In *The Histories*, Herodotus explained the purpose of this strategy: "The horse fears the camel and cannot abide the sight or the smell of it. . . . Indeed, as soon as the battle was joined, the very moment the horses smelled the camels and saw them, they bolted back; and down went all hope for Croesus."

The Persians then began a siege of Sardis, which lasted two weeks. (A siege means cutting off a town or fort from the outside so it cannot receive supplies and citizens cannot escape.) The siege forced Croesus to surrender, and Cyrus added Lydia to his empire. It took several years, however, for Persian generals to end rebellions in the region.

ON TO BABYLONIA

In the years that followed, Cyrus turned his attention to Babylonia. This would be his next military target, so he tried to win allies in the

IN THEIR OWN WORDS

I Am King of the World

In 538 B.C.E., Cyrus had scribes (people whose job is to write down all important records) write a description of his new government on a cylinder made out of clay. This Cyrus Cylinder was discovered by archaeologists in the 19th century. It offers some of the few documented clues about Cyrus's reign in Babylonia. The Cyrus Cylinder contains the only known words of Cyrus the Great. It was written in the Akkadian language. The cuneiform script covers a cylinder about 10 inches long and 5 inches wide. After describing the state of Babylonia under King Nabonidus, Cyrus spoke to the Babylonians:

I am Cyrus, king of the world, great king, mighty king, king of Babylon, king of Sumer and Akkad, king of the four quarters . . . When I entered Babylon in a peaceful manner, I took up my lordly

abode [home] in the royal palace amidst rejoicing and happiness . . . Marduk, the great lord, established as his fate for me . . . who loves Babylon, and I daily attended to his worship. . . . I sought the welfare of the city of Babylon and all its sacred centers. As for the citizens of Babylon, [upon whom] he [Nabonidus] imposed

The Cyrus Cylinder was written in 538 B.C.E. and explains Cyrus's history and the government he established.

region. The ruler, Nabonidus (r. 556–539 B.C.E.), had angered some of the Babylonian priests by turning away from the local god Marduk and accepting a new, foreign god. Cyrus received promises of support from some of these priests. A Babylonian general named Ugbaru (d. 538 B.C.E.) also promised to help Cyrus.

In 539 B.C.E., Cyrus made his move into Babylon. *The Babylonian Chronicles* describes how his forces killed many Babylonians in Opis, along the Tigris River. Then he turned on the city of Sippar, where Nabonidus was staying. The *Chronicles* say, "The 15th day, Sippar was seized without battle. Nabonidus fled. The 16th day, Gobryas [Ugbaru], the governor of Gutium, and the army of Cyrus entered Babylon without battle. Afterwards, Nabonidus was arrested in Babylon when he returned there."

a corvée which was not the gods' wish and not befitting them, I relieved their wariness and freed them from their service. Marduk, the great lord, rejoiced over [my good] deeds.

He sent gracious blessing upon me, Cyrus, the king who worships him, and upon Cambyses, the son who is [my] offspring, and upon all my army. . . .

Corvée means forced labor or slavery, so Cyrus was noting that he freed the Babylonians from slavery. He went on to describe his other good deeds:

I returned the images of the gods, who had resided there [in Babylon], to their places and I let them dwell in eternal abodes. I gathered all their inhabitants and returned to them their dwellings.

This part means Cyrus restored the old Babylonian gods that Nabonidus had ignored. He also let the foreigners who had been forcibly taken to Babylon return to their homes. This included tens of thousands of Jews, who had been forced from their homeland and sent to Babylon earlier in the 6th century B.C.E.

To some modern observers, Cyrus was a great champion of human rights. He ended slavery and let everyone worship as they chose. The Cyrus Cylinder has been called the first document that spells out the protection of human rights. Because of this, the United Nations has a copy of it in its New York headquarters. Some historians, however, point out that many Near Eastern kings before Cyrus began their rule by pointing out the ways they helped their citizens.

(Source: "Cyrus Cylinder (2)." Livius: Articles on Ancient History. Available online. URL: http://www.livius.org/ct-cz/cyrus_I/cyrus_cylinder2.html. Accessed February 15, 2008.)

Cyrus the Great's tomb can still be seen today in Pasargadae, Iran.

Cyrus waited several weeks before entering the city of Babylon, the capital of the country. When he finally arrived, he claimed the title of king of Babylonia and said the god Marduk had blessed his victory. This connection to the local god made it easier for the Babylonians to accept Cyrus as their ruler.

With the victory in Babylonia, Cyrus also won the loyalty of Syria, Palestine, and Phoenicia—all located along the Mediterranean Sea. The Phoenicians were particularly well known for their skills as sailors and shipbuilders, so for the first time the Persians had a navy.

Cyrus did not make great changes in how the Babylonians ran their affairs. Local people remained in charge of the government, under the control of a Persian satrap. Cyrus let the people worship any god they chose. The pattern of giving conquered people a good deal of freedom would continue under other Persian rulers.

After his victory in Babylonia, Cyrus turned his attention to the east. He may have already fought in eastern Iran and Central Asia, in the years before his Babylonian conquest. Details of his military actions in the east are hard to find. But it seems certain that he expanded the territory of the old Median Empire in the region beyond the Oxus River (now called the Amu Darya). This region was called Transoxiana, and included parts of what are now Afghanistan, Uzbekistan, Turkmenistan, Tajikistan, and Kazakhstan.

Along the Jaxartes River (now called the Syr Darya), Cyrus founded a new city, Cyropolis, most likely in what is now Tajikistan. Near there, according to Herodotus, the Persians fought in 530 B.C.E. against the Massagetae, who were a Scythian people. Cyrus had his men build boats to form a bridge across the Jaxartes River. On the other side, the Persians battled forces led by Massagetae Queen Tomyris (dates unknown). Cyrus had earlier kidnapped her son, who killed himself while in Persian hands.

In this battle with Tomyris, Cyrus was killed. His body was brought back to Pasargadae, where it was placed in a tomb that still stands today in the ruins of Pasargadae.

ON TO EGYPT

With the death of Cyrus, his oldest son, Cambyses, became the Great King. When he was alive, Cyrus had already given his son control of Babylonia. It was clear that he intended for Cambyses to one day rule the whole empire. Cambyses ended the military action in the east. Upon returning to Persia, he made plans to invade the only other Near Eastern empire remaining—Egypt.

The preparations for this invasion took four years. Cambyses strengthened the Phoenician navy, so it could battle the Egyptians at sea. Greek soldiers from Anatolia also joined the Persian army, and the island of Cyprus aided Cambyses. To prepare for his land invasion, Cambyses made a deal with Arabs who lived along the Sinai Desert. The Arabs agreed to provide water to the Persians as they marched across the hot sands on their way to Egypt. Camels would carry animal skins filled with the water.

Just as his father had done before attacking Babylon, Cambyses also won allies among his enemy's people. He convinced a Greek general to turn against his master, the Egyptian pharaoh (king) Amasis (r. ca. 569–525 B.C.E.). The general and his Greek troops were mercenaries (professional soldiers who fought for anyone who was willing to pay them). Cambyses also seemed to earn the support of Egyptian priests who opposed their pharaoh.

In 525 B.C.E., while both sides were still preparing for war, Amasis died. His son Psamtile III (r. 525 B.C.E.) then took control. But his rule did not last long. The Persians soon reached Egypt. They won a major battle outside Pelusium, near where the Nile River enters the Mediterranean. No details of the battle survive, but Herodotus wrote, "The battle was very fierce; many fell on both sides, and at last the Egyptians were defeated." The Greek historian said that, decades after the battle, he saw the piles of bones left by the dead soldiers.

With this loss, the pharaoh retreated to Memphis. Cambyses and his men were in pursuit. After a siege of the city, Cambyses defeated Psamtile and won control of Egypt. As he began his rule, a former

Cats as Weapons

According to some legends, Persian king Cambyses and his men were able to take the town of Pelusium in Egypt without using their weapons. They used cats instead. To the ancient Egyptians, cats were protected animals, since they were sacred to their goddess Bastet. The story goes that Cambyses released a number of cats into the town before his troops entered. Another version says that he had his men march with the cats in front of them. In either case, the Egyptians refused to attack the Persians because they were afraid of killing the cats, giving the Persians an easy victory. This story is sometimes credited to Herodotus, but it does not appear in *The Histories.*

Egyptian admiral and the pharaoh's personal doctor, Wedjahor-Resne (dates unknown), helped Cambyses behave like a true Egyptian king.

The Egyptians accepted Cambyses as the first pharaoh in a new ruling dynasty. But soon many priests turned against his rule. This is because Cambyses lowered the taxes collected to support the priests and the temples of the gods. That meant the priests had to do more for themselves.

Despite Wedjahor-Resne's praise, Cambyses is not portrayed well in most ancient history books. The priests' anger, as well as the Greek attitude that Persians were generally uncivilized, may have influenced what they wrote. Herodotus portrayed Cambyses as ruthless, and perhaps even crazy, when he ruled the Egyptians. Modern historians take a more balanced view. Kaveh Farrokh wrote in *Shadows of the Desert* that Cambyses, "like his father, respected conquered peoples and their customs."

The "Lost Army"

According to Herodotus, Cambyses sent 50,000 troops to Siwa Oasis (an area with water in the middle of a desert) in Egypt, perhaps to visit an oracle there. (An oracle was a priest or priestess who was said to be able to communicate with the gods and deliver messages from them.) On the way, a giant sandstorm buried the soldiers, and they were never heard from again.

This "lost army" has long intrigued scholars and explorers, who wonder if it really existed. And if it did, where are its remains buried? In 1935, a Hungarian explorer named Laszlo Almasy (1895–1951) tried to find Cambyses' army. He was convinced it had taken a route northward from another oasis in the desert. Almasy failed to find any traces of the Persians, but others continued to search the region.

In 2000, a team of Egyptian scientists was in the desert near Siwa looking for oil. They found bits of cloth, metal, and bones, and some people thought they were left by the lost army. Egyptian archaeologists explored the site, but no new findings have been reported. Still, that does not stop people, including tourists, from looking for the lost army.

INTRIGUE FOR THE THRONE

For several years, Cambyses tried to spread his control over more of North Africa. He took control of Libya without a fight, because the Libyans agreed to accept his rule. Persian troops fought in Ethiopia, gaining some lands there.

In 522 B.C.E., as Cambyses was finally going back to Persia, he died. (Herodotus claimed he accidentally stabbed himself with his own sword while getting on his horse.) Cambyses had no sons, so when he died, there was great confusion about who would rule next. The events surrounding this succession make one of the greatest mysteries in ancient Persian history.

Cambyses had a brother named Bardiya, known as Smerdis to the Greeks. By some accounts, Cambyses was returning to Persia because his brother had rebelled and claimed the kingship for himself. Other sources say Cambyses had secretly killed Bardiya several years earlier, before the invasion of Egypt. Still, someone named Bardiya was calling himself the true king of Persia. Who was it?

A Persian nobleman named Darius claimed he knew the answer. The man who called himself Bardiya was actually a magus—a priest in the Zoroastrian religion. Darius said this man's real name was Gaumata, and he was said to look just like Bardiya. Since Bardiya had been murdered secretly, the Persians did not know he was not really Cambyses' brother.

Most modern historians doubt this version of events. Most believe Bardiya was not murdered and did lead a rebellion to seize the crown from his brother. Or, Bardiya might have rightfully taken the throne after he learned of Cambyses' death. Since the king had no sons, Bardiya was next in line to be king. By some accounts, the Medes in particular accepted Bardiya. And the people in foreign lands under Persian control welcomed the tax cuts that he ordered.

In any event, Darius used his version of the truth to explain his actions. As he later wrote (quoted by Maria Brosius in *The Persians*), "No one dared say anything about Gaumata the magus until I came." With help from six other Persian nobles, Darius killed Bardiya at either Susa or in a part of Media called Nisaia in 522 B.C.E.

After taking power, Darius returned lands that he claimed Bardiya had taken from the people and restored temples the "false" king had destroyed. He also gave himself the title King of Kings—which was used by future Persian rulers.

Darius was the son of a satrap who ruled in Parthia. Before his attack on Bardiya, he had served in Egypt as a spear-carrier for Cambyses—a kind of personal guard for the king. This position meant he was probably a well-respected nobleman. But Darius was not a member of the royal family and had no direct ties to the former rulers of either Media or Persis. Still, Darius claimed he was entitled to be king because he had distant ties to Achaemenes, the founder of the first Persian ruling dynasty.

Most historians believe Darius did not have ties to Achaemenes, and that this legendary first Persian king may not have even existed. Darius might have created him to support his claim that he had a right to rule Persia. If that is true, the Achaemenid Empire, one of the world's greatest empires ever, was named for a man who never lived!

The Behistun Inscription

Darius recorded his version of history on the face of a steep mountain along the road between Babylon and Ectabana. The mountain is near the town of Behistun in modern Iran, and the writings on it are called the Behistun inscription. Darius had workers carve the story into the rocky cliff, along with a relief showing him defeating the false Bardiya. (A relief is a sculpture created by carving away the surrounding rock or other material to leave an image that rises off the background.)

The words are written in Elamite, Akkadian, and Old Persian. Darius claimed that he had scribes create the first cuneiform version of Old Persian just for this inscription.

The text of the inscription was also written on scrolls in Aramaic, a common language throughout the Near East at the time. Pieces of these scrolls have been found in Iraq and Egypt.

In the inscription, Darius claimed that Ahura Mazda, the Persian god, had chosen him to be king. The false Bardiya had not only tried to destroy the legal ruling dynasty, but he also ruled harshly. Darius wrote (as quoted at Livius.org), "The people feared him exceedingly, for he slew [killed] many who had known the real Smerdis [Bardiya]. For this reason did he slay them, 'that they may not know that I am not Smerdis, the son of Cyrus.'"

REBELS IN THE KINGDOM

In the years to come, with the help of the six nobles who supported him, Darius expanded the empire he now ruled. First, however, Darius had to end several rebellions that broke out after he took power. Several rebels claimed to be king, and people in the distant reaches of the empire thought the troubles in the Persian heartland would offer a chance to win their independence.

The unrest spread farther out, beyond Mesopotamia and Media. Eventually it reached Persis and regions to the north and west—Armenia, Bactria, and Parthia. Darius himself led troops against the rebels, while his father and some of the six trusted nobles led other armies. Tens of thousands of rebels were killed or taken prisoner.

Finally, just a little more than a year after coming to power, Darius and his supporters ended the various rebellions. Darius would now begin a career that would lead to his being known through history as Darius the Great.

CHAPTER 2

THE ACHAEMENID EMPIRE AT ITS LARGEST

DARIUS PROVED HIS SKILLS AS A MILITARY LEADER BY defeating the rebels within his growing empire. In the decades to come, he would show his talents as a political leader as well. Cyrus the Great founded the Persian Empire, but Darius the Great strengthened it and expanded it. Under Darius, the Persians created a strong central government that lasted for more than 150 years.

Darius seems to have paid more attention to affairs in the provinces than Cyrus and Cambyses had. He turned to experts in the various satrapies for advice. In a few places, he also made sure that local laws were written down, and he encouraged quarreling groups within the empire to settle their differences with treaties rather than violence.

Darius also introduced the first Persian coins, which were used throughout the empire. The new gold coin was the *daric* and the silver coin was the *sigloi*. They replaced the old coins from Lydia, which had been used for decades.

A GREAT BUILDER

Like most rulers, Darius wanted concrete signs of his greatness and power. He began several huge building projects. One was in Susa and another was in a new capital city called Persepolis. Susa, the old capital of the kingdom of Elam, had been destroyed by the Assyrians during the 640s B.C.E. Darius built a new palace there, called the Apadana, or Audience Hall. Susa was his first capital and it seemed to be his favorite. Herodotus wrote about it, and it is also mentioned in the Bible, while neither text mentions Persepolis.

OPPOSITE
Darius built several huge buildings, including a palace at Persepolis. This relief from the palace shows him on his throne.

The Eyes of the King

Communication was often slow and difficult in ancient times, and Darius and the Persian satraps could not have direct knowledge of everything that happened in the empire. To keep track of his citizens, Darius hired special inspectors. The Greeks referred to them as the "King's Eyes," or "Eyes and Ears." These inspectors were somewhat like spies, keeping track of events in the kingdom and then reporting back to Darius. The use of these informers seems to date back to the Median kings of old. The King's Eyes made sure tributes were collected, and they watched for any signs of rebellion in the satrapies. The Greeks later borrowed this government role for themselves, calling the informers "overseers."

From Susa, Darius improved the Royal Road that ran to Sardis in Lydia. Several roads connected key cities in the empire, and Darius built a series of posts along the roads where riders could rest and change horses during their journey.

Starting around 518 B.C.E., Darius built his capital at Persepolis. He had his workers build a huge, flat stone surface about 45 feet above the plain. Large steps led up to this plateau. On it, Darius built a grand palace and other buildings. At the great hall, called the Apadana, stone columns as tall as a modern five-story building towered over Darius and the guests he welcomed. Work on the buildings at Persepolis continued long after his death.

NEW CONQUESTS

Darius was not merely a great builder. Like both Cyrus and Cambyses before him, the new Great King sought to expand his empire. Around 520 B.C.E., he launched an invasion against a Scythian tribe known as the "pointed-hood" Scyths, because of the tall caps they wore. They lived east of the Caspian Sea in what is now Turkmenistan.

Some historians suggest these Scyths had helped some of the rebels in the Central Asian satrapies who had challenged Darius's rise to the throne. Rather than attack his enemy head on, Darius used boats to bring his troops across the southeast corner of the Caspian Sea. Darius claims to have killed many of the Scyths, including their chief. He then appointed another man their chief to gain control of the province.

Around 518 B.C.E., Darius pushed the empire farther eastward by taking land in India. There are no details of the battles he fought there or of the exact borders of the Indian Empire. But Persian influence extended to the Indus River, in what is now Pakistan. The region became a rich source of gold for the Persian Empire.

After spending time in the east, Darius turned his attention toward Europe. In 513 B.C.E., he gathered an army of as many as 150,000 men. He also relied on a navy of 600 ships, sailed by Greeks from Persian lands in western Turkey. To enter Europe, Darius linked these boats together to form a floating bridge. The bridge let his land forces cross the Bosporus, the narrow waterway that separates Europe from Asia south of the Black Sea.

The Persians entered Thrace, where the people accepted Persian rule rather than fight. To the west, Macedonia also came under Persian control. Darius then headed north and crossed the Danube River, in modern-day Romania, on his way to fight the Scyths. Herodotus says the Scyths were outmatched by the larger Persian army, so they used a "scorched earth" approach. They retreated, destroying crops and closing wells, so the Persians would not have food and water as they marched.

Since the Scyths were nomads, they were used to moving constantly. But Darius grew tired of chasing them, especially since his men lacked food and water. He returned to his "bridge" at the Bosporus and went home. He left the general Megabazus (dates unknown) in charge of the Persian troops that remained in Thrace.

The ruins of the palace of Persepolis, built by Darius and Xerxes.

THE GREEKS REBEL

For more than a decade, Darius kept his troops home and life in the empire was fairly peaceful. But in 499 B.C.E., trouble erupted in Asia Minor. Aristagoras (d. 497 B.C.E.), the ruler of the Greek city-state of Miletus, encouraged several other Greek city-states that were under Persian rule to rebel. He also sought aid from Athens, one of the major Greek city-states on the mainland of Europe, as well as the smaller city-state of Eretria.

In 498 B.C.E., the Greek rebels attacked Sardis, the most important city in the region. For the next six years, Darius worked to regain control. In some cases, he won back their loyalty without a fight. But in Miletus and other city-states, the Persians had to restore their control on the battlefield.

When the fighting ended, Darius punished the mainland Greeks who had aided the rebels. The Persians had become more active in the area around the Mediterranean Sea. The major Greek city-states, particularly Athens, were natural rivals for Persia if the Great King wanted to expand his presence in the Aegean and Mediterranean Seas. Darius wanted to show the Athenians they should not interfere in Persian affairs or challenge his power.

In 490 B.C.E., a Persian army invaded independent Greece. The soldiers destroyed buildings on the island of Naxos, then headed for

IN THEIR OWN WORDS

Building the Susa Palace

To build his new palace in Susa, Darius brought in supplies and workers from across his empire. An inscription he left on this palace describes how he built the royal palace and imported products from all over his empire.

This palace which I built at Susa, from afar its ornamentation was brought. Downward the earth was dug, until I reached rock in the earth. When the excavation had been made, then rubble was packed down, some 40 cubits in depth, another part 20 cubits in depth. On that rubble the palace was constructed. . . .

The cedar timber, this was brought from a mountain named Lebanon. The Assyrian people brought it to Babylon; from Babylon the Carians and the Greeks brought it to Susa. . . .

The gold was brought from Lydia and from Bactria, which here was wrought. The precious stone lapis lazuli and carnelian which was wrought here, this was brought from Sogdia. The precious stone turquoise, this was brought from Chorasmia, which was wrought here.

The silver and the ebony were brought from Egypt. The ornamentation with which the wall was adorned, that from

Greece was brought. The ivory which was wrought here, was brought from Nubia and from India and from Arachosia.

The stone columns which were here wrought, a village named Abiradu, in Elam—from there were brought. The stone-cutters who wrought the stone, those were Greeks and Lydians.

The goldsmiths who wrought the gold, those were Medes and Egyptians. The men who wrought the wood, those were Lydians and Egyptians. The men who wrought the baked brick, those were Babylonians. The men who adorned the wall, those were Medes and Egyptians.

Darius the King says: At Susa a very excellent work was ordered, a very excellent work was brought to completion. . . .

A cubit is a unit of measurement about equal to the length of a person's forearm. *Wrought* means worked or manufactured using hand tools.

_____

(Source: "Darius' building inscription from Susa." Livius: Articles on Ancient History. Available online. URL: http://www.livius.org/da-dd/darius/darius_i_t03.html. Accessed June 25, 2008.)

the city-state of Eritrea. After six days of fighting, local people who opposed their rulers opened the gates of their city to let in the invading Persians. Many residents of Eritrea were forced to go to the Persian city of Elam as punishment for resisting the Persian conquest.

Then the Persians turned south, toward Athens. They landed outside the main city at the Bay of Marathon. From there, some 20,000 troops marched to a nearby plain. For several days, the Persian and Athenian armies watched each other across the plain of Marathon. When the fighting began, Persian arrows rained down on Greek infantry (soldiers who fight on foot). The infantry, however, known as hoplites, stood close to one another with their shields locked together. This formation (called a phalanx) kept most of the arrows from hitting the Greek soldiers. The Greeks were able to get close to the invading Persians and use their greater skill in hand-to-hand combat.

Herodotus wrote in *The Histories* that these Athenians were the first "to charge their enemy at a run and the first to face the sight of the Median dress and the men who wore it. For till then, the Greeks were terrified even to hear the names of the Medes." But the Athenians fought bravely and forced the Persians to retreat. As the Persians fled back to their ships, the Greeks followed them and continued fighting, leading to even more deaths.

In *The Persian Empire*, Lindsay Allen writes that compared to other battles, the Persian loss at Marathon was not a major one. But for the Greeks, Allen says, "the encounter's effect on Greek ideas about their own identity, distinct from the peoples of Asia, was enormous." The Greeks began to see themselves as the defenders of freedom and democracy. For them, the Persians represented the harsh rule of kings. An idea of "the West" (Greece, and later, Rome) and "the East" (Persia) as opposing cultures grew out of the battles between the Greeks and Persians.

XERXES AND THE GREEKS

In 486 B.C.E., Darius the Great died and his son Xerxes (ca. 519–465 B.C.E.) became the King of Kings. According to inscriptions he left at Persepolis (quoted in Allen's *The Persian Empire*), Xerxes had several brothers, "[But] thus was the desire of Ahuramazda [the Persian god]: Darius, my father, made me the greatest after himself."

Scythian Heavy Cavalry

Either the pointed-hood Scyths or other related peoples of the steppes were among the first fighters to develop what is called heavy cavalry. Riders wore heavy suits of armor and helmets and fought with lances (long, pointed weapons) and swords. Light cavalry used less armor and were better suited for scouting missions of raids, but not for going into battle against large armies. The Persians adopted the heavy cavalry for their armies, and the Greeks and Romans later learned from the Persians the value of these well-protected riders. Heavy cavalry was a feature of Western warfare until the 18th century.

Like his father, Xerxes added new buildings in Persepolis. He also faced revolts in Egypt and Babylonia soon after taking power. He crushed them both. But for the first years of his rule, Xerxes had one main goal: invade Greece to punish the Athenians for their victory at the Battle of Marathon.

Xerxes made careful plans for this invasion. Food was collected and left in several spots in Thrace, so his advancing troops would not go hungry. His engineers built another floating bridge to connect Asia and Europe, this time at the Hellespont, near the Aegean Sea. Xerxes also assembled a navy of more than 1,200 war ships, and perhaps 3,000 more vessels helped carry troops and supplies. His army numbered around 100,000 soldiers. By comparison, only 20,000 to 30,000 had taken part in the first invasion of Greece in 490 B.C.E.

Xerxes' massive army was an international force. Parthians, Scyths, Bactrians, and others from the steppe joined the Medes and Persians as the main cavalry force. They fought with lances, bows and arrows, and

Uncovering Xerxes' Canal

To prepare for his invasion of Greece, Xerxes had workers dig a canal near Mount Athos, which sits on a peninsula (an area of land surrounded by water on three sides) south of Macedonia. During the 490 B.C.E. invasion, Persian ships had trouble going around the peninsula, and Xerxes did not want a repeat of those difficulties. The canal would eliminate the need to go around.

Herodotus wrote that men from many nations were forced to dig the canal, which was about 1.25 miles long. In recent times, some historians doubted the canal was real or that it really cut all the way across the peninsula.

In 2001, a team of researchers proved that the canal did exist, that it crossed the entire peninsula, and that it was wide enough to let two ships pass. No remains of the canal are visible today, but technology used to find underground resources such as petroleum and minerals allowed researchers to map the canal's location.

They believe the canal was built solely for Xerxes' invasion and was not used again. At their Web site, "The Canal of Xerxes in Northern Greece," the researchers wrote that this lack of later use "suggests that Xerxes built the canal as much for prestige and a show of strength as for its purely functional role."

swords. The infantry included Lydians, Egyptians, Assyrians, and Babylonians. Their weapons included a variety of bows, swords, and spears. Some Libyan forces rode in chariots, while a few Arabs launched arrows while riding camels. At sea, Phoenicians sailed the ships, with Persians or Medes in command.

For this invasion, Xerxes led the troops himself. In the Persian tradition, the Great King commanded his forces from a central point on the battlefield, surrounded by 10,000 royal guards carrying spears. These special soldiers were the best in the army, and traveled with their own wagons that carried their women and supplies.

Before setting out on his march to Greece, Xerxes had issued an order. He demanded that the Greek city-states send him earth and water—a sign of their loyalty to him. But Athens and Sparta refused to accept Xerxes' power, and they prepared for war.

This silver and gold bowl shows archers who may have been members of the royal guard known as the Immortals.

THE SECOND GREEK-PERSIAN WAR

The first battle in 480 B.C.E. was located at Thermopylae, a pass along the shore of the Gulf of Malis so narrow that only one chariot could pass through at a time. On the southern side of the track stood the cliffs, while on the north side was the gulf. Greek troops waited there to stop the Persians from advancing toward Athens.

The defenders included 300 of the best Spartan warriors, led by their king, Leonidas (d. 480 B.C.E.). For the first attack, Xerxes sent several thousand soldiers into the region. But the narrow space between the water and the mountains prevented them from using their advantage in manpower. The Greeks also had longer spears and could easily stab the Persians. Even the Persian royal guards could not beat the Greeks.

Several days passed, and a Greek traitor finally told Xerxes about a secret path his men could use to surround the defenders at Thermopylae. Following this advice, the Persians advanced. The Greeks realized

The Immortals

According to Herodotus, the 10,000 royal guards were called the Immortals, because as soon as one was killed, he was immediately replaced by another soldier. However, of the ancient historians who wrote about Persia, only Herodotus referred to them as the Immortals. One historian suggests Herodotus may have confused the Persian word for "immortals" with the word for "companions." Later Greek historians, writing after the reign of Alexander the Great, describe an elite Persian army unit called the Apple Bearers. They carried spears with a metal apple (or pomegranate) attached to the end of the handle, to help balance the weight of the spear. The Apple Bearers and the Immortals were most likely the same unit.

the Persians would soon be marching on the Greek city-states to the south. They left to protect the rest of Greece.

Leonidas stayed behind with his Spartans and some soldiers from other city-states. Their task was to hold the Persians off while the Greeks got ready to defend their homelands. Leonidas was greatly outnumbered and all his soldiers were eventually slaughtered. But not before they made a heroic stand and held the Persians off for two days.

While the Persians were at Thermopylae, their navy was fighting a Greek fleet. The two navies met at Artemisium, off the island of Euboea in the Aegean Sea. Neither side won a clear victory, but a storm destroyed many Persian ships.

Back on land, the victory at Thermopylae gave the Persians an easy route through Attica to Athens. Most of the citizens there had already fled the city. The Persians then advanced on the Acropolis—a hill where the main temples in the city stood. They defeated the Athenian troops defending the temples. They also stole many art treasures from the buildings on the Acropolis and from other temples in the city. Then the Persians burned buildings in the almost-empty city.

Modern historians have suggested that destroying Athens did not serve a military purpose. Xerxes simply wanted to punish the Athenians for their refusal to accept Persian dominance. However, it is important to remember that looting and burning a conquered city was a common practice in the world at that time. Xerxes did punish the Athenians, but he also ensured that they would have a lasting hatred for the Persian invaders.

The Persians lost the next major battle of the war, a naval conflict near Salamis. This island, west of Athens, was close to the Greek mainland. The Greeks tricked the Persian ships into entering the narrow strait (a narrow passage of water connecting two larger bodies of water) between the island and the mainland. They were then able to destroy a large portion of the Persian fleet.

Xerxes thought about waging one more naval battle, but rejected the idea. He wanted the remaining ships to return safely to Asia Minor so he could use them again. As the Great King prepared to return to Sardis by land, he left the general Mardonius (d. 479 B.C.E.) in charge of 10,000 top troops.

Mardonius and his men stayed among their Greek allies in Thessaly. The Persian general tried to improve relations with the Athenians by offering to rebuild the temples the Persians had destroyed. The Athenians refused, and they prepared for another battle. In 479 B.C.E.,

Athens, Sparta, and their allies defeated Mardonius's army at Plataea, near the border of Attica. The key to the Greek victory was unity. The Greeks were not a united nation, and each city-state functioned independently. But when they were faced with a common threat, they were able to fight together.

Plataea marked the largest battle the Persians fought on land in Europe. It was also their last on the continent. After the Greek victory, Xerxes and his successors never tried to conquer European lands again.

TROUBLE AT HOME

One reason Xerxes returned home in 479 B.C.E. may have been to end another rebellion in Babylonia. In general, however, the empire remained mostly peaceful during and after the Greek war. Xerxes used

---

IN THEIR OWN WORDS

The Battle of Thermopylae

The Persians did not leave many records of their battles. Or if they did, they have not survived. So the details of the Greek-Persian war come mostly from Herodotus, who recorded this description of the fighting at Thermopylae.

> Now they joined the battle outside of the narrows, and many of the barbarians fell; for behind their regiments their captains with whips in their hands flogged on every man of them, pressing them ever forward. Many of them, too, fell into the sea and were drowned, and even more were trampled to death by their comrades . . . the Greeks, knowing that their own death was coming to them from the men who had circled the mountain, put forth the very utmost strength against the barbarians; they fought in a frenzy, with no regard to their lives.

> Most of them had already had their spears broken by now, and they were butchering Persians with their swords. And in this struggle fell Leonidas, having proved himself a right good man, and with him other famous Spartans. . . . On the Persian side . . . there fell, among many other distinguished men, two sons of Darius. . . .

Herodotus clearly favors the Greeks in his account. For example, he refers to the Persians as "barbarians," which means uncivilized people. He also says the Persian soldiers were whipped by their captains to force them to fight—implying that they were cowards. A Persian description of this battle would probably have told a very different story.

(Source: Herodotus. *The History*. Translated by David Greene. Chicago: University of Chicago Press, 1987.)

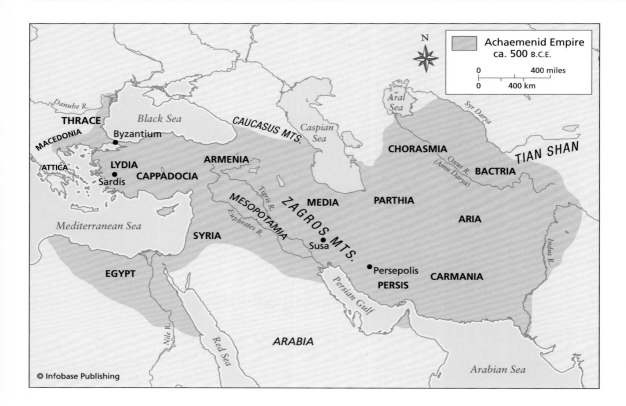

Under the Persian king Xerxes, the Achaemenid Empire stretched across the Middle East and into Egypt.

the vast riches he gathered from his subjects to build new palaces in Persepolis and the other imperial capitals, and the government seems to have run smoothly. But despite the calm in the empire, trouble stirred close to home for Xerxes. The Great King died in 465 B.C.E., probably killed by one of his own sons.

The Greek author Ctesias (fifth century B.C.E.) claimed that a Persian noble teamed with a palace advisor to kill Xerxes. The killers then blamed the murder on one of the king's sons, Darius, who had already been picked by Xerxes to be the next king. Another of the royal sons, Artaxerxes I (r. 465–425 B.C.E.), then killed Darius for his supposed crime and became king. Artaxerxes then learned about the two men who had killed his father and executed them. Many modern historians do not accept this version of events, but they believe some kind of palace rivalry and murder led to Artaxerxes becoming his father's successor.

The Greek historian Plutarch (ca. 46–120 C.E.), in his *Lives*, called Artaxerxes, "[A]among all the kings of Persia the most remarkable for a gentle and noble spirit." When he first came to the throne, Artaxerxes faced several rebellions. One in Bactria ended quickly. But in Egypt, fighting dragged on for several years. The rebels there had help from Athens in the form of 200 warships. Artaxerxes sent a large army to destroy the fleet of ships, and Egypt was once again firmly under Persian control.

Athens' involvement in Egypt came after the Athenians had created their own empire in the Aegean. They were the strongest of a group of allied city-states. Athens tried to gain territory by taking it away from Persia. When Xerxes was king, the Athenians had attacked Persian posts in Asia Minor. They destroyed ships and took riches back to Athens. The growing strength of Athens posed a danger to the Persians in the western part of their empire.

But instead of fighting each other again, the two powers tried to work out an arrangement. According to the Treaty of Callias, signed some time around 449 B.C.E., Persia agreed to stay out of the Aegean Sea and Athens recognized Persian control over the lands of Asia

CONNECTIONS

The Book of Esther

Susa is the setting for the Book of Esther, from the Old Testament of the Bible, and Xerxes is one of the major players. The events described in the Book of Esther take place primarily in Shushan, which is the capital of King Ahasuerus's empire. Shushan is the Hebrew form of Susa and Ahasuerus's name in Greek is Xerxes.

According to the story, Ahasuerus argued with his first wife and decided to take another one. He married a Jewish woman named Esther, who kept her religion a secret from him. After Esther had been queen for several years, Ahasuerus appointed the Persian Haman to be his prime minister. Haman ordered that everyone should bow to him, but Esther's cousin Mordecai refused because it was against Jewish law. As punishment, Haman decided to kill all the Jews in Shushan.

Mordecai told Esther about Haman's plan. Like all queens of Persia, she was not allowed to see Ahasuerus unless he called for her. But, risking death, she went to the Great King. She revealed that she was Jewish and asked him to spare her people. Ahasuerus agreed. Haman was killed and Mordecai became an official in Ahasuerus's court

Ahasuerus/Xerxes was certainly a real person, and there are Persian stories about a Jewish queen of Persia. Still, some historians are not sure the story is true. Nevertheless, today Jews celebrate the holiday of Purim to honor Esther and Mordecai.

In this silver statue, a
Persian official wears
the typical clothes of a
traveler.

Minor. The Greek city-states and Asia Minor would be free to run their own affairs.

Modern historian A. R. Burns, in the *Cambridge History of Iran*, writes that the two peoples, Greek and Persians, were also "getting to know each other as human beings." Herodotus, for example, tried to understand Persian culture and habits, and the Persians must have learned about Greek customs, religion, and culture.

TAKING SIDES IN GREECE

Toward the end of Artaxerxes' rule, the Greeks actually saw Persia as a potential ally. Sparta and Athens were now rivals in a struggle to control Greece, and each wanted to win the support of Persia. The conflict between Sparta and Athens lasted from about 431 to 404 B.C.E. and is known as the Peloponnesian War. Artaxerxes, however, did not choose sides and he died in 424 B.C.E.

His son Xerxes II (d. 424 B.C.E.) became the next Great King. But within 45 days he was killed by his half-brother, who was then killed by another half-brother, Nochus (d. 404 B.C.E.). Nochus declared himself king and took the name Darius II. During his reign, Persia became heavily involved in Greek affairs.

At first, Darius renewed the old treaty with Athens. But around 420 B.C.E., the Athenians angered the Great King by supporting a rebellion in Lydia led by the satrap, Pissouthnes (d. after 420 B.C.E.). A Persian general named Tissaphernes (d. 395 B.C.E.) seems to have bribed the Athenians so they would drop their support of Pissouthnes, and the rebellion ended. Darius then had Pissouthnes executed.

In the years to come, Athens continued to support other rebels in the Persian Empire. In the meantime, Sparta was gaining the advantage in the Peloponnesian War. But it still needed help. The Athenian activities in Lydia may have convinced Darius that he could not trust them. Whatever the reason, Darius decided to help Sparta.

In 413–412 B.C.E., Tissaphernes led diplomatic talks with Sparta. At the same time, he tried to see if he could make a better deal with the Athenians, but they refused. Tissaphernes ended up signing the first recorded treaty between Sparta and Persia.

Thucydides, in *The History of the Peloponnesian War*, recorded three different versions of the treaty. The last is the one both sides

Thucydides and the Persians

Modern historians consider Thucydides to be more accurate than Herodotus in recording ancient events. His only known work is *History of the Peloponnesian War.* For a time, Thucydides commanded Athenian troops during that war. He only wrote about a small part of the Persian Empire and how their actions related to Greek affairs. But Thucydides offered details that were lacking in Persian and other sources of the era. He is still read today by historians and teachers looking to understand the meeting of Persian and Greek cultures in the fifth century B.C.E. His work is taught at military colleges and to students of modern international relations.

totally accepted. In part, it said, "The Spartans and their allies shall not go against the King's Country [Persia] with any hostile intent; not shall the King [Darius II] go against the country of the Spartans and their allies with any hostile intent." If any Persian satraps attacked the Spartans, Darius was supposed to stop them. Tissaphernes also agreed to pay for local ships to help the Spartans, until Darius could send another fleet. And Tissaphernes and the Spartans would have to agree on any treaty to end the war with Athens.

Tissaphernes failed to deliver the Persian navy he promised. The Spartans soon learned they could not trust him. Darius wanted stronger aid for his new allies, so in 407 B.C.E. he sent his son Cyrus the Younger (ca. 424–401 B.C.E.) to Asia Minor to direct the Persian effort. Cyrus, by some accounts, was just 16 years old at the time. But he had already proven himself to be a skilled soldier. Cyrus also offered some of his personal wealth to help the Spartans fund their war against Athens. With the increased Persian aid, the Spartans and their allies won the war.

CIVIL WAR IN PERSIA

By 404 B.C.E., Cyrus was back in Susa, standing at his father's bed as he lay dying. Darius had already named Cyrus's older brother, Artaxerxes II (r. 404–358 B.C.E.), as the next Great King. Tissaphernes told Artaxerxes that Cyrus wanted to kill him so he could become king. The two sons' mother then stepped in, asking Artaxerxes to pardon his brother. The new Great King did forgive Cyrus, and Cyrus went back to his satrapy in Asia Minor. The younger brother, however, was soon planning a rebellion.

In Sardis, Cyrus began recruiting an army. This included 14,000 Greek mercenaries who had sharpened their skills during the Peloponnesian War. With the peace in Greece, these soldiers were now available to fight for Cyrus in Asia.

Cyrus said he needed an army to fight a mountain tribe in his satrapy, but Tissaphernes knew he was lying. He and others advised Artaxerxes to build an army to fight his brother. The king, however, acted slowly. Plutarch, in his *Lives*, wrote that one advisor told the king he "ought not to avoid the conflict, nor to abandon Media, Babylon, and even Susa, and hide himself in Persis, when all the while he had an army many times over more numerous than his enemies."

Finally, in 401 B.C.E., Artaxerxes sent a force westward to meet his brother.

Meanwhile, Cyrus had marched his men across Turkey toward Mesopotamia. Most of his troops had not been told they were about to fight the forces of the Great King of Persia. As they marched, however, they realized Cyrus's plan and were not happy. Many of the mercenaries wanted to go home.

Cyrus needed to win their support. The Greek mercenary and historian Xenophon (ca. 431–ca. 352 B.C.E.) wrote in *Anabasis* (a book about Cyrus's expeditions), "Cyrus promised to give them all half as much they had been getting before"—from one gold *daric* a month to one and a half. However, he still refused to admit that he planned to fight his brother the king.

The men marched on for several more weeks, and finally met Artaxerxes' army. The battle took place near the Euphrates River at a place

Xenophon and the Ten Thousand

Xenophon was one of the mercenaries Cyrus hired for his rebel army. He wrote a book about his experience that is commonly called *Anabasis* (it is also sometimes translated as *The Expedition of Cyrus* or *The Persian Expedition*). It provides an eyewitness account of the march into Mesopotamia. But today, the book is best known for the story it tells after Cyrus's loss at Cunaxa.

Xenophon was one of the generals who led the surviving 10,000 Greeks through the mountains of Asia Minor on their way back home. This story of "the Ten Thousand" has been called one of the greatest adventures recorded in ancient times. The Greeks battled local people, difficult climate, and harsh weather on their way to the Black Sea and the Greek mainland. Hundreds of years later, the Romans marveled at the march of the Ten Thousand, and modern scholars still do.

Anabasis is a Greek word that means "march up country." The word is sometimes used today in English, too, to describe any long, difficult military march or retreat. Xenophon's tale has also inspired several modern fictional works. These include the 1979 movie *The Warriors,* which sets the tale among rival street gangs in New York City. Several novels have been written on the topic that have the title *The Ten Thousand*. These include one in 2001 by Michael Curtis Ford and one in 2008 by Paul Kearney.

called Cunaxa, about 70 miles north of Babylon, in modern-day Iraq. Cyrus had about 30,000 men—about half as many as the king's army.

Artaxerxes commanded his troops, surrounded by the royal guards. Cyrus and his men were able to break through the royal guards, and the two brothers fought one another. According to Plutarch (who was citing another historian), Cyrus first wounded Artaxerxes' horse, but the king quickly found another. Cyrus then attacked again, knocking the king to the ground.

Cyrus then charged his older brother, but Artaxerxes and his men threw javelins (light spears) at him. Another version says Cyrus fell during the fight and smashed his head on a rock. In either case, Artaxerxes defeated his brother and ended the rebellion. According to Xenophon in *Anabasis*, the Persians lost a great leader that day at Cunaxa. He said of Cyrus, "Of all the successors of Cyrus the [Great], no Persian was a more natural leader and none more deserved to rule."

MORE REBELLIONS

Since the time of Darius the Great, the borders of the Persian Empire had remained fairly stable. Rebellions broke out, but the Great Kings were always able to stop them or work out arrangements with the local rulers.

Artaxerxes, though, faced huge challenges after his defeat of Cyrus. Just a year after his victory, Persia was once again fighting the Spartans in Asia Minor. The Persians were able to drive out the Spartans. In 386 B.C.E., in an agreement that came to be known as the King's Peace, the Spartans and other Greeks once again pledged to stay out of Asia Minor.

Egypt had also been in rebellion for several years and the rebellion did not end well. In 385 B.C.E., Artaxerxes sent a force to regain control, but the Egyptians defeated it. More than a decade later, the Great King tried again to conquer the Egyptians, and again he failed. The Egyptians now had full independence from Persia.

In what is now northern Iran, a people called the Cadusians also troubled Artaxerxes. These nomads lived in the Elburz Mountains, south of the Caspian Sea. From the time of Darius the Great, they had occasionally resisted Persian rule. Artaxerxes personally led an expedition against them into the mountains.

Then, in 368 B.C.E., the first of several western satraps declared their independence from Persia. Sometimes they had the support of the Spartans and other Greeks. Artaxerxes was able to end the various rebellions, but the Persians were relying more than ever on Greek mercenaries to fight their battles. This made them vulnerable, for they had plenty of enemies in Egypt and the Aegean looking to weaken them.

As the Great King grew old, he knew his sons were competing to be his successor. Each had the support of different nobles. Artaxerxes died in 359 B.C.E. His oldest son, Darius, should have been the next king, but he was killed by his brother Ochos, who took the name Artaxerxes III (d. 338 B.C.E.). According to Plutarch (writing in *Lives*), the new Persian ruler was "hot and violent" and "outdid all his predecessors in bloodthirstiness and cruelty." He proved this by having a role in the death of two other brothers to secure his place as king.

Like his father, Artaxerxes III faced rebellions in Asia Minor. These he crushed. He also sent troops to Egypt in about 353 B.C.E. to try to bring it back into the Persian Empire. This effort failed. Then several more revolts broke out in Phoenicia, along the Mediterranean coast. Artaxerxes ended these. Then, once again, he sent troops into Egypt in 343 B.C.E., leading them himself. This time, his soldiers defeated the Egyptians. Egypt was once again part of the Persian Empire.

THREAT FROM THE WEST

Artaxerxes III died in 338 B.C.E. Diodorus of Sicily, who wrote in the first century B.C.E., says a palace advisor killed the king and most of his family, then arranged for a surviving son to rule as Artaxerxes IV (d. 336 B.C.E.). Some modern historians, however, question this claim. There is a Babylonian source that suggests Artaxerxes died of natural causes.

His successor, however, was clearly the victim of a palace coup (a quick and violent takeover) in 336 B.C.E. With his death, Codommanus emerged as the new Great King. He was a distant Achaemenid family member. The new king took the name Darius III (d. 330 B.C.E.).

By this time, Persia faced a new threat from the Greek world. Macedonia had thrown off Persian rule decades before. It was now a growing kingdom ruled by a strong king, Philip II (382–336 B.C.E.).

In 340 B.C.E., Philip had attacked the city of Perinthos (modern-day Marmara Ereglisi), near the Hellespont. The Greek city was an ally of Athens, which was resisting Philip's efforts to take over all of Greece. Artaxerxes sent forces to fight him, and Athens also joined the war against Macedonia. The two allies defeated the Macedonians.

However, Philip soon brought the Greek city-states under Macedonian rule. For some time, Philip had been preparing for an attack on the Persian Empire. The Persians had invaded Greece 150 years earlier, causing much destruction. They still ruled several eastern Greek cities. Philip considered his neighbor to be a constant threat to the Greeks. In 337 B.C.E., the Greeks under Philip agreed to declare war on the Persians.

Philip was the supreme commander of the combined Greek and Macedonian forces. He sent about 10,000 soldiers to attack the coast of Asia Minor in the spring of 336 B.C.E. His plan was to join this force and lead the charge into Persia. But before he could do so, he was murdered. Leading the invasion of Persia now fell to Philip's son, Alexander.

ALEXANDER THE GREAT

It took Alexander two years to gain complete control of his own empire in Greece, but by 334 B.C.E., at the age of 22, he was ready.

Alexander and some 37,000 troops crossed the Hellespont and landed in Asia Minor. They joined up with an advance force of Macedonians that Philip had sent before he died. As they marched, a Greek mercenary named Memnon began preparing the Persian forces. The two armies met at the Granicus River.

Although the Greeks were outnumbered, they excelled in hand-to-hand combat. Alexander was also a brilliant general. He soon defeated the Persians. By some accounts, several thousand Persians died, including three members of Darius's family. Alexander lost only 100 men.

Alexander then marched south down the Aegean coast of Asia Minor, then headed east. Meanwhile, Darius began to gather a huge army and prepared to meet the Greeks. The Great King himself led this force, which numbered more than 100,000 soldiers. Coming from Babylon, the Persians met the Greeks in 333 B.C.E. at a town called Issus (a coastal plain between what is now Turkey and Syria).

Darius ignored the advice of some of his advisors, who wanted to fight the Greeks in an open plain. With plenty of room, Darius could use his larger army and skilled cavalry to his advantage. But when the battle came, the Persians were hemmed in by the sea and mountains and lost their advantage. Darius, surrounded by his royal guards, fought bravely. But he realized he could not defeat Alexander and retreated.

In the confusion of the battle, members of the Persian royal family were taken prisoner by the Greeks. Darius wrote to Alexander, asking for their return. Alexander refused and told Darius he now considered himself the king of all Asia. The Greeks were not even close to the Persian heartland, but Alexander's words would soon be true. He turned his forces south, conquering Phoenicia and Egypt, then headed for Mesopotamia.

Darius saw his opponent's strength. He wrote Alexander a second time, offering money for the safe return of his family. He also said he would let the Macedonian king rule all the land up to the Euphrates River, and Darius would rule east of it. Alexander rejected this proposal. Darius then built another massive army, knowing time was running out to save his empire.

In October 331 B.C.E., the two armies met at Gaugamela, near the city of Arbil in what is now Iraq. Once again, the Greek and Macedonians proved their skill. According to the Greek historian Arrian (ca. 86–160 C.E.) in his *Anabasis of Alexander*, Darius fled early in the battle, leaving behind riches and weapons. He then "marched through the mountains of Armenia towards Media . . because he thought Alexander would take the road to Susa and Babylon . . . [which] appeared to be the prizes of the war."

Alexander the Great conquered the Persian Empire and put an end to the Achaemenid dynasty.

The Great King was right. Alexander went to those two cities, taking the wealth stored in them. Alexander proclaimed himself the king of Persia. He then marched to Persepolis, where he destroyed the royal buildings begun by Darius the Great almost 200 years earlier. Alexander said this destruction was revenge for the Persian destruction in Athens in 480 B.C.E.

In the Elburz Mountains, Darius tried to raise an army to fight Alexander one more time. The eastern satraps, however, saw how weak Darius was. In 330 B.C.E. one of them, Bessus (d. 329 B.C.E.), the satrap of Bactria, killed the Great King. Alexander had been chasing Darius for a long time, but when he finally caught up with him, the Persian king was dead.

Bessus proclaimed himself the king of Persia, but Alexander the Great, the Macedonian, was the true king now. Other satraps came over to his side. Alexander continued pushing eastward until he reached India. The Achaemenid dynasty had ended, and so had the first great Persian Empire.

CHAPTER 3

THE NEW PERSIAN EMPIRES

ALEXANDER THE GREAT DIED IN 323 B.C.E. WITH NO CLEAR successor. His generals spent the next 40 years fighting among themselves. Alexander's huge empire soon split into smaller kingdoms.

A Macedonian general named Seleucus took control of the central part of the old empire. He set up a capital, Seleucia, near Babylon, and ruled lands that stretched from Asia Minor through present-day Afghanistan. But he was murdered before he could achieve his ambition of grabbing the throne of Macedon as well. His kingdom was continued by his successors. At its largest, the Seleucid Empire stretched from the Aegean Sea to Central Asia.

Seleucus and the kings who came after him kept many local Persian officials in place. They also continued to control their empire by breaking it up into satraps. The Seleucids established many Greek settlements throughout their lands. Some of the Persian officials became Hellenized, meaning they adopted the language and culture of the Greeks. (The term comes from *Hellas*, the word the ancient Greeks used to mean the entire Greek world; this is also what Greeks today call their nation.) But most people continued to speak Persian, Aramaic, and other languages of the old empire, and they kept their old ways of life.

The Seleucid Empire lasted more than 240 years. But it continually lost territory over the years because of wars and rebellions. The Seleucid rulers often battled invading nomadic tribes. They also fought in Egypt, which was ruled by another Hellenistic dynasty, the Ptolemaic dynasty. In 246 B.C.E., another war with Egypt enabled Greek generals to seize power in the Persian satraps of Bactria and Parthia. The Greek Bactrians ruled their own wealthy kingdom for more than 100 years.

OPPOSITE

A Parthian horseman. The Parthian Empire arose in Persia about a century after the defeat of the Achaemenids.

The Parthians gradually captured all the Seleucid territories east of Syria. Parthia eventually became the heart of a new Persian Empire.

THE RISE OF PARTHIA

Just before the revolts in Bactria and Parthia, a nomadic tribe from central Asia called the Parni had settled in Parthia. They spoke a form of Persian. They also shared the nomadic culture of the other people who had come before them to the Iranian Plateau. The Parni settled around the city of Asaak (near the modern Iranian city of Kuchan). They adopted the local form of Persian spoken in Parthia, and later became known as Parthians. Details about the Parthians are scarce, partly because they left fewer inscriptions than the Achaemenids did.

The Parni set up their own local kingdom, and around 247 B.C.E. Arsaces (r. 247–217 B.C.E.) became the king. He founded the Arsacid dynasty. Its descendants would become the rulers of the Parthian Empire. The Roman historian Justin (third century C.E.) wrote in his *Epitome of the Philippic History* that Arsaces was "a man of uncertain origin, but of undisputed bravery." The details of his life and rise to power are not clear. But it seems Arsaces led a revolt against the local

Coins minted by the Parthian kings offer some of the best historical evidence of their reigns. This is a silver coin showing Mithridates I.

satrap, who had already begun his own revolt against the Seleucids. Arsaces defeated the satrap. This gave him control over all of Parthia. He then moved west and took control of the neighboring satrap, Hyrcania. For a time, the Seleucids gained the upper hand, forcing Arsaces to flee Parthia. But he regrouped his forces and won back the territory.

Under Mithridates I (r. 171–138 B.C.E.), Parthia emerged as a true power. Mithridates took the throne in 171 B.C.E., and within several years had expanded his empire into parts of Bactria. Around 148 B.C.E., he pushed westward and took Media and then advanced on Babylonia. As his empire grew, however, Mithridates struggled to control it. When nomads struck from the northeast, he had to send troops there to protect his borders. This gave the Seleucids the chance to retake Mesopotamia.

LOOKING BACK, MOVING FORWARD

Mithridates died in 138 B.C.E. His successors would continue to struggle with the same problems he had faced: nomads on one side and the Seleucids on the other. Scyths who were forced out of their lands by Central Asian nomads rampaged across Parthia. At one major battle around 128 B.C.E. they defeated the Parthians.

The Seleucids also made one last attempt to regain Babylonia. The Arsacids, however, asserted their control there. They were also finally able to coexist with the Scyths. The Scyths eventually settled in lands near modern-day Pakistan and became known as the Indo-Parthians.

In 123 B.C.E., Mithridates II (r. ca. 123–87 B.C.E.) came to power. He was the first Arsacid king to make a link between his family's rule and the Achaemenids of old. Mithridates took the title Great King, and he left carvings documenting his deeds at Behistun, just as Darius the Great had done four centuries earlier. But Mithridates, and the Arsacids who followed him, never built a strong central government the way Darius and his successors had. Local rulers throughout the Parthian Empire had a great deal of freedom, and nobles had a say in choosing the new kings.

Mithridates II strengthened Parthia's rule on both its eastern and western borders. His conquests extended Parthian power north and west of Babylonia—parts of Mesopotamia it had not controlled before. He founded the city of Ctesiphon, near Babylon, and within several decades it became the new Parthian capital. This location in

History Through Coins

Coins minted by the Parthian kings offers some of the best historical evidence of their reigns. The coins help historians learn the names and dates of the rulers. The coins also have images of the kings' faces. Parthian coins are still being uncovered by archaeologists working in Iran and neighboring countries. They offer new clues about the empire's history. The coins are also popular with collectors, which has led to some modern criminals creating counterfeit coins. In 2001, a coin expert in England declared that some gold and silver coins said to be from Parthia were actually fake.

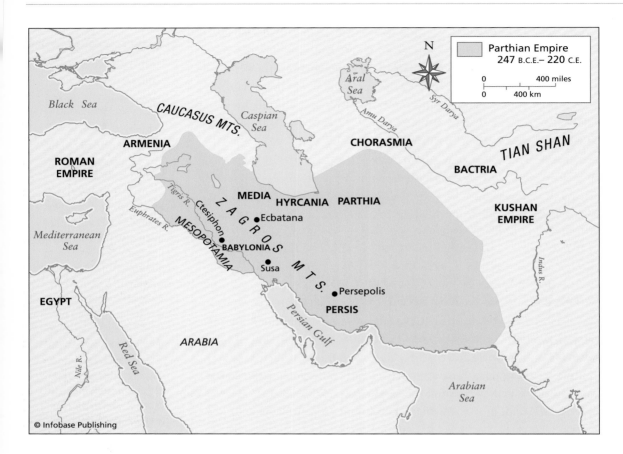

Parthian Empire
247 B.C.E.– 220 C.E.

© Infobase Publishing

Parthian kings were able to strengthen the borders of the empire and move further into Mesopotamia. Parthia and China also began a trade route that became known as the Silk Road.

Mesopotamia helped link the Parthians to the great empires of the past. Ctesiphon was also a safer spot than the old capital in Hyrcania, which nomads could easily raid. The Great King also strengthened ties with the Indo-Parthians, giving Parthia influence east of its own boundaries.

Around 97 B.C.E., Mithridates II took control of Armenia, which had been mostly independent under the Seleucids. The Great King had already kidnapped an Armenian prince, Tigranes (ca. 140–55 B.C.E.). Now Mithridates II had him installed as king of Armenia.

Tigranes was the son-in-law of Mithridates VI Eupator (ca. 132–63 B.C.E.). Mithridates VI Eupator ruled Pontus, a kingdom in Asia Minor south of the Black Sea. (The name *Eupator* is Greek for "of a good father.") After the fall of the Achaemenid Empire, that region had kept some of its Persian culture, and also blended it with Hellenic culture.

Mithridates II married a daughter of Tigranes, which cemented his alliance with Armenia. Then, to strengthen himself even further, he formed an alliance with Tigranes' father-in-law, Mithridates VI Eupator.

Around the same time, the Romans and Parthians made their first diplomatic contact. By now Rome had replaced Greece as the dominant power in the Mediterranean. In 96 B.C.E., the Roman general Sulla (138–78 B.C.E.) was in Asia Minor fighting the Pontians. A Parthian diplomat met Sulla at the Euphrates River. The two men talked, and most likely reached an agreement that the Euphrates River would be the line that divided their political interests.

But according to Plutarch in his *Lives*, Sulla treated the Parthians with "vulgarity and ill-timed arrogance." Sulla gave the diplomat the same status as the leader of Cappadocia, which was a small kingdom in Asia Minor. Mithridates II believed a Parthian should have received better treatment, and took Sulla's action as an insult. He executed the diplomat for tolerating it. In the years to come, Rome and Parthia were destined to clash over lands they both wanted to control—Mesopotamia and Armenia.

After Mithridates II died in ca. 87 B.C.E., several kings who were not Arsacids managed to rule Parthia for a time. The Arsacids returned to power in 70 B.C.E., when Phraates III (r. 70–57 B.C.E.) took the throne. By this time, both Armenia and Pontus were in conflict with Rome. In 69 B.C.E., Mithridates VI Eupator and Tigranes asked Phraates to help them battle the Romans. At the same time, the Romans told Phraates to stay out of the conflict. Phraates remained neutral, and Rome defeated Mithridates VI Eupator and Tigranes.

THE BATTLE OF CARRHAE

At this time, the Roman general in Asia Minor and Mesopotamia was Lucullus (ca. 117–ca. 56 B.C.E.). After his defeat of Armenia and Pontus, he thought about breaking the old agreement that Rome would not cross the Euphrates River. As Plutarch writes in his *Lives*, the general was drawn to the idea of "making his way, unvanquished [undefeated] and victorious, through three of the greatest empires under the sun." His troops, however, refused to go farther east. War with Parthia would have to wait.

Meeting the Chinese

The rise of Parthia as an Asian power drew the attention of another empire—China. In 121 B.C.E., a Chinese diplomat visited Mithridates II to establish ties between the two empires. A Chinese official wrote (as quoted by Maria Brosius in *The Persians*) that the Great King "ordered [a general] to take a force of 20,000 cavalry and welcome them at the eastern frontier." Mithridates then sent his own diplomats to China, who brought ostrich eggs as a gift. These ties led to trade between Parthia and China, and eventually opened a trade route known as the Silk Road that stretched from China all the way to Europe.

CONNECTIONS

An Ancient Medicine

Mithridates VI Eupator enters the pages of Persian history because of his ties to Parthia and his conflicts with the Roman Empire. The king is also known for creating an antidote—a drug that stops the effects of a poison. The king feared that his enemies would try to kill him with poison, so he experimented with different herbs, seeds, and other substances that could work as antidotes. He tested the poisons and possible antidotes on prisoners and slaves before finding one combination that seemed to work. It was later called *mithridatum* in his honor.

The drug was used for almost 2,000 years, and was also known as theriac. It was made up of various herbal substances mixed with honey. Various formulas emerged, based on what was available in each region where the drug was made. Greek physician Galen (129–200 C.E.) devoted a whole book to theriac. One of his patients, Roman emperor Marcus Aurelius (121–180 C.E.), took it regularly. Eventually, theriac formulas found their way to China. Pharmacists throughout Europe sold it as late as the 1880s.

In 66 B.C.E., Pompey (106–48 B.C.E.), another Roman general, sent troops east across the Euphrates River. King Phraates asked the Romans to obey their agreement not to cross, and diplomacy ended the problem. Still, as modern historians Beate Dignas and Engelbert Winter write in *Rome and Persia in Late Antiquity*, "Rome . . . was convinced of its political, military cultural superiority over the East."

A few years later, the Arsacids of Parthia had family struggles for power that mirrored the conflicts the Achaemenids sometimes faced. Around 57 B.C.E., Phraates' sons Orodes II (r. ca. 57–38 B.C.E.) and Mithridates III (d. 55 B.C.E.) killed their father. The two brothers then battled one another for power. Orodes' forces were finally able to capture Mithridates in 55 B.C.E. Justin wrote that Mithridates trusted his brother would treat him well. Instead, "Orodes, contemplating him rather as an enemy than a brother, ordered him to be put to death before his face."

By this time, a Roman army led by Crassus (ca. 115–53 B.C.E.) was on its way from Syria. Crassus may have heard reports of Mithridates' early success and wanted to help him fight his brother. Or perhaps he thought the rebellion put Orodes in a weak position and he would not be able to defend his kingdom. In either case, Crassus wanted to invade Parthia for the glory and wealth it would bring him.

Crassus began his attack in 54 B.C.E. by crossing the Euphrates River and taking control of lands in northern Mesopotamia. He returned to Syria for the winter to gather more troops, then headed back to Babylon and the nearby Seleucia in the spring of 53 B.C.E. Crassus was confident he could take Babylon and the nearby city of Seleucia. But a Parthian diplomat warned him not to be so sure. As quoted by the ancient Roman historian Cassius Dio (ca. 150–ca. 235 C.E.) in his *Roman History*, the Parthian held out the palm of his hand and said, "Sooner will hair grow here than you shall reach Seleucia."

While Crassus built his army and prepared to cross the Euphrates again, Orodes assembled his own forces. As in the days of the Achaemenids, the cavalry was the heart of the Persian army. Light cavalry with archers rode into battle first, followed by the heavily armored cavalry that rode with long lances. Their horses wore armor too—plates of bronze and steel. When the Roman soldiers heard about the Parthians' heavy armor and powerful weapons, Plutarch said in his *Lives* that they lost their courage: "[N]ow, contrary to their hopes, they were led to expect a struggle and great peril."

The Parthians relied mostly on their cavalry, trying to avoid hand-to-hand combat. The Romans, like the Greeks before them, counted on their infantry and close combat to defeat their enemies. One Parthian battle tactic was to have the light cavalry pull away from the enemy, as if they were leaving the battle. Then, the archers would fire as they rode away, giving the enemy no chance to return fire. The Parthians may have adapted this tactic from the Medes or Scyths, and it became known as a "Parthian shot."

In 53 B.C.E., Orodes led his army against the Romans. The

The Roman Empire

From its start as a small Italian village covering seven hills, Rome grew to become one of the largest, most powerful empires of all time. Spreading out from their homeland, the Romans seized power in all directions in Europe. They also conquered in North Africa and Asia, taking over lands that had once been part of the Achaemenid Empire.

The Romans found a worthy enemy in Persia. They first clashed with the Parthians in 53 B.C.E. The two empires continued to battle each other, on and off, for almost 250 years.

The Sassanians then took up the battle on the Persian side. As the western half of the Roman Empire began to crumble, the eastern half, called Byzantium, kept up the struggle into the seventh century C.E.

Although they were often enemies, the Romans and Persians traded with each other, and some Romans worshipped gods who first appeared in Parthian lands. The works of several ancient Greek and Roman historians give us the Roman view of the Parthians and the Sassanians. Unfortunately, the Persians left behind almost nothing about their side of the conflict and how they viewed the Romans.

two armies met near the city of Carrhae (also known as Haran), in what is now southeast Turkey. Orodes had 1,000 heavy cavalry and 9,000 archers on horses. Behind them, 1,000 camels carried extra arrows and other supplies. His men faced up to 42,000 Roman soldiers, and were

IN THEIR OWN WORDS

No Escape

Here is a Roman and a Greek view of the Battle of Carrhae (fought in 53 B.C.E.). The first is by Cassius Dio, from his *Roman History*, written in the early third century C.E. He describes the deadly effects of the Parthian archers. (*Mortal* means deadly. Here, the word *missiles* means the arrows the Parthians shot.)

The missiles falling thick upon them [the Romans] from all sides at once struck down many by a mortal blow, rendered many useless for battle, and caused distress to all. They flew into their eyes and pierced their hands and all the other parts of their body and, penetrating their armor, deprived them of their protection and compelled them to expose themselves to each new missile. Thus, while a man was guarding against arrows or pulling out one that had stuck fast he received more wounds, one after another. Consequently it was impracticable for them to move, and impracticable to remain at rest. Neither course afforded them safety. . . .

In this selection from *Lives* (written about 75 C.E.), Greek historian Plutarch describes Roman efforts to fight back against the Parthians. (The Gauls were natives of what is now France, and they had already come under Roman control. Publius was the son of Roman general Crassus.)

Publius himself, accordingly, cheered on his cavalry, made a vigorous charge with them, and closed with the enemy. But his struggle was an unequal one both offensively and defensively, for his thrusting was done with small and feeble spears against breastplates [armor] of raw hide and steel, whereas the thrusts of the enemy were made with pikes against the lightly equipped and unprotected bodies of the Gauls. . . . For they laid hold of the long spears of the Parthians, and grappling with the men, pushed them from their horses, hard as it was to move them owing to the weight of their armor; and many of the Gauls [got off] their own horses, and crawling under those of the enemy, stabbed them in the belly. These would rear up in their anguish, and die trampling on riders and foemen [enemy soldiers]. . . .

(Sources: Cassius Dio, *Roman History*. Lacus Curtius. Available online. URL: http://penelope.uchicago.edu/Thayer/E/Roman/Texts/Cassius_Dio/home.html. Accessed February 12, 2008; Plutarch, *Lives*. Lacus Curtius. Available online. URL: http://penelope.uchicago.edu/Thayer/E/Roman/Texts/Plutarch/Lives/home.html. Accessed March 2, 2008.)

heavily outnumbered. But the Romans proved to be no match for the Persian archers and cavalry.

As night fell, the surviving Romans left their camp to seek shelter behind the city walls of Carrhae. After spending one night there, they began to retreat. About half the Roman soldiers had been killed in the fighting, and the Parthians took another 10,000 prisoner. Modern historian A. D. H. Bivar, writing in the *Cambridge History of Iran*, says the defeat showed "Parthia as a world power equal, if not superior, to Rome." With the victory, the Euphrates River was now the firm boundary between the Roman and Persian worlds. Armenia again promised its loyalty to the Parthians.

MORE CONFLICTS WITH ROME

The Battle of Carrhae was part of a centuries-long struggle between the Romans and Persians to control Mesopotamia, Armenia, Syria, and nearby lands. After the victory at Carrhae, Orodes sent troops into Syria, but this and another invasion in 38 B.C.E. did not give the Parthians control of the region.

The next Great King, Phraates IV (r. 38–2 B.C.E.), soon faced another Roman invasion. This one was led by Mark Antony (ca. 83–30 B.C.E.). As many as 100,000 Romans, foreign allies, and mercenaries marched through Armenia and entered Media. Phraates was able to destroy some of the machinery the Romans used to attack towns, such as battering rams (heavy objects swung or rammed against a door or wall to break it down), catapults (large machines used to hurl heavy objects at an enemy), and towers placed against city walls so soldiers could attack. Antony's Armenian allies deserted him, and the Parthians eventually drove him off. A treaty in 20 B.C.E. once again set the Euphrates River as the boundary between the Roman and Parthian Empires.

With peace at hand—at least for a time—the Arsacids faced troubles in their own court. Around 10 B.C.E., Phraates IV sent four of his sons to live in Rome. The Great King may have wanted to protect the boys from any possible violence at the royal court. Perhaps the move indicated his desire for good relations with Rome. They were treated well at the court of Augustus (63 B.C.E.–14 C.E.), the first Roman emperor. Some Romans, however, thought the arrival of the princes was a sign that the Parthians were bowing to Roman power. They considered the sons to be hostages.

Phraates had a son with a woman who was an Italian slave and had been a gift from Rome. He chose this son, Phraates V (r. 2 B.C.E.–4 C.E.)

Defeated by Illness

When the Romans captured Ctesiphon in 164, illness played a part in finally driving them out. A deadly disease, perhaps smallpox, had spread to Babylonia from the east. The Roman soldiers were likely first exposed to it in the town of Seleucia, and it quickly spread among the army. Although it struck the Parthians too, the Romans had less natural resistance to the disease, and they died in large numbers. The losses played a part in Rome's decision to leave Parthia. The soldiers then carried the sickness back with them to Rome, killing many more people.

Fighting with the Romans, led by Emperor Trajan, weakened the Parthians. Eventually, they were replaced by another powerful Persian dynasty, the Sassanians.

as his successor. The Parthian nobles disliked having a king with a foreign parent, and they grew angrier when Phraates V married his own mother. In 4 C.E., the nobles killed the king and backed Orodes III (r. 4–7) as the new ruler.

One of the other sons, Vonones (r. ca. 7–ca. 12), then came back from Rome to rule Parthia. To the Persians, however, he seemed too Roman and had lost his ties to Persian culture, so the nobles forced him from power.

After several years of turmoil, Artabanus II (r. ca. 11–38) took power. Rome and Parthia had peaceful relations for most of his rule. Under Vologeses I (r. 51–ca. 77), who took the throne in 51, Persia reasserted its control over Armenia. This led to another war with Rome. In 63, the two empires agreed to share control over Armenia. This peace lasted for more than 50 years.

But Rome still wanted to expand to the east by taking over Parthian territory. In 114 the Roman emperor Trajan (ca. 53–117) invaded Armenia. From there he turned south and entered Babylonia. He took the Persian capital of Ctesiphon without a fight; the Great King Osroes (r. ca. 108–ca. 137) had already fled.

Trajan reached the shores of the Persian Gulf, and perhaps thought of going even farther, but trouble was stirring behind him. The people of the conquered lands were rising up against the Romans. In 117, while on his way back to Rome, Trajan died.

His successor, Hadrian (76–138), gave back most of the Persian lands Rome had just conquered. He realized it would be too hard to control lands so far from the center of Roman power. Still, Rome had gained influence in Armenia at Parthia's expense, and it kept some land in northern Mesopotamia.

Two more times during the second century Roman troops stormed Ctesiphon: in 164 and 198. Each time they withdrew, but only after either damaging royal palaces or looting the government treasury. Parthia had some successes of its own, invading Roman lands in Syria and Asia Minor. But the Parthians could never hold their gains.

Parthia's last great military triumph against Rome came in 217. The year before, the Roman emperor Caracalla (188–217) invaded Parthia. According to Dignas and Winter in *Rome and Persia in Late Antiquity*, the emperor was "guided by the idea that he would become the successor of Alexander the Great." Instead, he was murdered. The new emperor, Macrinus (ca. 164–218), led the invasion.

The Parthian king Artabanus IV (r. 213–224) led an army that met the Romans at Nisibis (modern Nuysabin, in southeastern Turkey). According to the Greek historian Herodian (ca. 170–ca. 240), in his *History of the Roman Empire*, the Persians used camels as well as horses in their cavalry and fought bravely. After two days of fighting, the battlefield was littered with bodies from both sides. Herodian wrote, "[T]he Parthians . . . stood their ground and renewed the struggle after they had carried off their dead and buried them." Finally, Macrinus asked for peace and agreed to give Artabanus money and gifts.

ONE EMPIRE FALLS, ANOTHER RISES

The years of war with Rome and fighting in the royal family weakened Arsacid power in Parthia. Local nobles amassed great wealth and land. Officials called *shahrdars* (similar to mayors) and *shahryars* (governors) had almost total control over the lands they governed. The Parthians had also let separate kingdoms exist within their empire, and one of these proved fatal to Parthian rule.

In Istakhr, the capital of the kingdom of Persis, a local ruler named Papak came to power around 205. After his death, his son Ardashir took control and began to extend his rule throughout Persis. Ardashir was the grandson of

CONNECTIONS

Shahs Today

In Persian, *shah* means king. The word serves as the root for *shahrdar* and *shahryar*, the titles of the officials who began to assert their power at the end of Parthian rule. As recently as the 1970s, the leader of Iran was known as the shah. Today in Iran and other countries where Persians once lived, *Shahryar* is sometimes used as a first name. *Shah, Shahrdar,* and *Shahryar* appear as family names as well. For example, in the early 2000s, Ishaq Shahryar was Afghanistan's ambassador to the United States.

a Zoroastrian priest named Sassan, and this name was used for the dynasty Ardashir founded.

From Persis, Ardashir and his armies began to attack other small kingdoms in the region. Ardashir also built a new city, which he named for himself. This activity caught the attention of the Parthian king, Artabanus IV. In 224 he led his soldiers into battle against Ardashir and the Sassanians.

A rock relief carved at Firuzabad, in south central Iran, shows Artabanus and Ardashir fighting a duel on horseback. Each king has a lance. Ardashir killed the Parthian king, then led his army westward to claim control of Parthia. Fighting went on for several years, because some Parthian leaders resisted Ardashir. But by 226, the Sassanians controlled the Parthian capital of Ctesiphon and Ardashir referred to himself as the King of Kings.

The Sassanians did not have much direct knowledge of the first great Persian Empire established by the Achaemenids. But they knew that Persis had been the home of the Achaemenids, and the Sassanians saw themselves as part of a great Persian tradition. They began to call their lands Eranshahr, or Empire of the Aryans, to strengthen that link to the past.

That link to the past led Ardashir into conflict with the Roman Empire. The Roman historian Herodian wrote that the Sassanian king wanted to take back all the lands that had once been under Persian rule. In his *History of the Roman Empire*, Herodian said the Roman emperor Severus Alexander (ca. 208–235) warned Ardashir that he "would find fighting against the Romans not the same thing as fighting with his barbarian kinsmen and neighbors." The emperor's

CONNECTIONS

The First Joust

In his book *Shadows in the Desert*, modern historian Kaveh Farrokh says the lance duel between Artabanus and Ardashir was the first of its kind. In ancient times, great warriors were known to fight one-on-one. The Sassanians, however, seem to have created rules for this kind of warfare, which they always fought on horseback with lances. The winning soldier won not just for himself, but for his army. The forces on both sides accepted that the winner of the duel was the winner of the whole battle.

These rules also applied later to lance duels, called *jousts*, between Sassanians and Romans. Jousting remained a part of combat in Asia and Europe for centuries, and was later turned into a sport. Instead of trying to kill an opponent, riders simply showed their skills with a lance on horseback. Jousting matches are still held today, and jousting is the official state sport of Maryland.

warning did not frighten Ardashir, and he launched a series of raids on Roman lands.

Rome responded with an invasion in 231. The Romans won some early victories, but they were stopped from taking Ctesiphon in 233. The Romans did take back the lands Ardashir had taken. Then they withdrew, claiming they had won the conflict. Modern historians think neither side won, because neither side gained new territory.

Within several years, however, the Sassanians had captured several Roman cities in Mesopotamia. Ardashir's successor, Shapur I (r. ca. 241–ca. 272), extended the gains even farther west. Rome won back some of these cities, then tried once again to take Ctesiphon. Shapur successfully defended the Sassanian capital.

Shapur I, the Sassanian king, successfully battled the Romans. He built a large tomb complex for himself at Naqsh-e Rostam, near Persepolis. This carving from Naqsh-e Rostam shows the defeated Roman emperor Valerian kneeling at Shapur's feet.

In an inscription he had carved in rock at Naqsh-e Rostam, near Persepolis (and quoted by Maria Brosius in *The Persians*), Shapur said, "a great frontal battled occurred . . . and the Roman force was destroyed." The war ended with Rome paying money to Shapur and giving up control of some lands in Armenia.

Peace never lasted long between Shapur and the Romans. In 252 C.E. they were fighting each other in Syria. The next year they fought in Turkey. Ancient records report that tens of thousands of soldiers were killed or captured in single battles. For the Sassanians, the Roman prisoners included one emperor, Valerian (d. ca. 260), who was captured at Edessa and died shortly after. More important to the Sassanians were Roman engineers and scholars, who were sent to live in Persis and other areas. They brought Roman skills and knowledge to Persian lands.

Shapur died around 272 C.E. Several of his sons served as king after him. One of them, Narseh (r. 293–302), launched an invasion against the part of Armenia that was under Roman control. By 298 C.E., however,

New Inscriptions Linked to Old

Shapur I tried to make a direct link to the Persian kings of old with his inscriptions at Naqsh-e Rostam, near Persepolis. The writings were near the tombs of some of the first Achaemenid rulers, including Darius the Great. Shapur wrote in three languages, just as Darius did with the inscriptions he left at Behistun. But Shapur used Middle Persian, Greek, and Parthian. Darius had used Old Persian, Akkadian, and Elamite. Also like Darius before him, Shapur claimed to have received authority from the god Ahura Mazda. Shapur went even farther, however, claiming he and his family traced their roots to ancient gods. Shapur said he wrote down his deeds (as translated by R. N. Frye in *The History of Ancient Iran*) "so that whoever comes after us may know this fame, heroism, and power of us."

the Romans had the upper hand and managed to capture Narseh's wife, sisters, and children. To end the war, Narseh agreed to give the land back to Rome in exchange for his family.

RELIGION AND WAR

The two rival empires managed to stay at peace for almost 40 years. When the fighting began again, religion was partly to blame. In 313 the Roman emperor Constantine (ca. 285–337) formally established freedom and toleration for all religions, including Christianity. Christians in Persia felt new ties to the Roman Empire and its Christian emperor. Shapur II (r. 309–379), the Sassanian king at the time, began to suspect the Christians in his empire might not be loyal to Persia.

Decades earlier, Shapur I had generally allowed religious freedom. So had the Achaemenids and Parthians before him. Zoroastrianism was the official state religion, but other faiths were accepted. These included Christianity, which arose in Roman lands during the first century, and Manichaeism, which developed in Persia during the third century.

For a time under Shapur I's sons, Zoroastrian priests tried to weaken other religions. Under Shapur II, though, things became much worse. Persian Christians were targeted for arrest or death, since they were seen as possible enemies of the state.

Constantine was preparing to battle the Persians when he died in 337. With the Roman emperor's death, Shapur invaded Armenia. This sparked another decades-long series of wars with Rome. Under the emperor Julian (r. 361–363), Rome invaded Babylonia in 362 and tried once again to take Ctesiphon. The attack failed and Julian was killed. The Romans agreed to give back the lands they had won under Constantine.

The reign of Shapur II marked the greatest extent of Sassanian power. He ruled for 70 years—longer than any other Sassanian king. He strengthened the power of the central government. He built forts and defensive walls along the edges of the empire, and brought distant lands under his direct control. The king made laws and oversaw the bureaucracy (the layers of officials that keep any government running). Still, the nobles and the Zoroastrian priests did play a part in Sassanian governments. A king needed their approval when choosing his successor.

For a time after Shapur II died, the nobles asserted some of their power. They helped force the end of the rule of Ardashir II (r. 379–383). He was replaced by Shapur III (r. 383–388) who was forced out in 388. Bahram IV (r. 388–399) took his place.

While the Sassanians struggled to find a suitable ruler, they managed to keep peace with Rome. Both the Romans and the Sassanians had new worries: They faced attacks by various tribes on their frontiers.

The Roman Empire was now split into two halves. The eastern half, which bordered Persian lands, was called Byzantium or the Byzantine Empire. Sassanian kings continued to persecute Christians in their lands, and some fled to Byzantium for safety. In 421, the Sassanian king Bah-

CONNECTIONS

Armenian National Pride

Although the Armenian Christians lost the Battle of Avarayr in 451, some of them continued to battle the Persians. They worked in small groups, hit important targets, then ran to the safety of the mountains. In 484, the Persians signed a peace treaty and let the Armenians worship as they wished.

To Armenians today, the Battle of Avarayr is a symbol of their people's courage in fighting for their faith. Vardanants Day (named for Vardan Mamikonyan, an Armenian military commander killed in the Battle of Avarayr), an important national holiday, commemorates the bravery of these fighters and the sacrifices they made.

ram V (r. 421–439) demanded that the Byzantine emperor send these Christians back to Persia. When he refused, Bahram started a war. It lasted only one year, but it signaled more conflict to come between Persia and Byzantium.

Religion also fueled more fighting with Armenia, where Christianity was the official religion. In 449, Yazdagird II (r. 439–457) of Persia called on his Christian subjects in Armenia to convert to Zoroastrianism. Many Christians then rebelled, and they asked Byzantium for help. The Romans, however, were too busy fighting the Huns and other invaders to send troops. In 451, the Armenians suffered a terrible loss against the Persians at the town of Avarayr, and many Christian priests and nobles were taken prisoner.

DECADES OF TROUBLE

Starting in the 440s, a Central Asian people called the Kidarites appeared on Persia's eastern borders. They joined the Hephthalites, or White Huns, as potential enemies. Yazdagird built forts along the border and pushed back the Kidarites.

But during the reign of King Peroz (r. 459–484), the Sassanians fought a series of wars with both the Kidarites and Hephthalites. Peroz was captured by the Hepthalites in 465, and later lost his life battling them. In the last decades of the fifth century, the Hephtha-lites had enough influence in Persia to play a role in choosing its new kings.

The constant invasions from Central Asian nomads were both a curse and a blessing. The Byzantine Empire was also being frequently invaded. Otherwise, they might have attacked Persia from the west and brought down the Sassanian Empire.

This gold, crystal, and garnet dish shows Khosrow, the last Sassanian king.

Peroz died in 484 and the Sassanians faced a new threat at home. A Persian named Mazdak (fifth century) had developed a new religion. Mazdak called for all wealth to be shared by everyone and said all Persians were equal. These ideas threatened the Zoroastrian priests, the nobles, and the wealthy, who did not want to give up their riches or power.

King Kavad (r. 488–496 and 499–531), however, supported Mazdak. The king saw some benefit to himself if the nobles and the priests lost some of their influence. Those powerful groups then forced Kavad from the throne in 496. But he returned three years later with an army and took back the kingship. In the years to come, Kavad turned against the followers of Mazdak, believing they threatened social order in the empire.

Kavad ruled for more than 30 years. During that time he battled the Byzantine Empire several times, as well as nomads to the north of his empire. His son Khosrow I (r. 531–579) took over in 531 and continued the wars with Byzantium. Khosrow is best remembered today for changes he made in the empire. He improved how taxes were collected and rewarded government officials for good service. He also improved communications and roads and began new building projects. Khosrow also supported the arts and education. He was considered the last great Sassanian king and was given the name of Anushirvan—"he of the immortal soul."

THE END OF THE EMPIRE

During Khosrow's reign, a new Central Asian power emerged—the Turks. The king had a son whose mother was a Turkish princess—a relationship meant to create a link between the Persians and the Turks. The Turks helped the Sassanians fight the Hephthalites in 560. But in the years that followed, the Turks made trade deals with the Romans and became an enemy of Persia.

Khosrow's half-Turkish son, Hormizd IV (r. 579–590), was king when the Persians and Turks clashed in 589. Hormizd's son, Khosrow II (r. 590–628), ruled when the Sassanians made some of their last major military gains. Persia once again conquered Syria and part of Egypt, and took Byzantine lands almost up to Constantinople.

In the end, however, neither the Turks nor the Byzantines posed the greatest danger to Persia. For several centuries, the Sassanians had dealt with tribes living across the Persian Gulf, on the Arabian Peninsula. At times, the Persians and Arabs battled each other. Other times, the two peoples were allies.

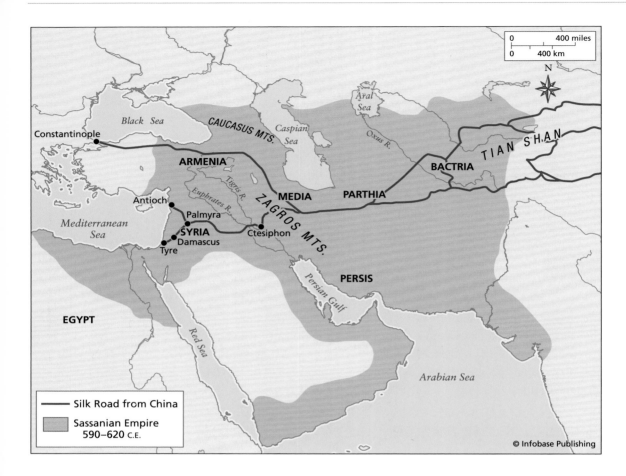

Silk Road from China

Sassanian Empire
590–620 C.E.

© Infobase Publishing

The influential Sassanian Empire dominated the Middle East and parts of southwestern Central Asia. The empire eventually fell to the Arabs in the seventh century, who moved eastward into Persian lands.

By the 630s, Arabs who had converted to the new religion of Islam became a major military power in southwest Asia. From their homeland in what is now Saudi Arabia, they began to conquer surrounding lands so they could spread Islam. They attacked Byzantine lands first, then moved into Persia.

In 637, Arabs seized the Sassanian capital of Ctesiphon. They kept moving eastward, taking Persian lands. In 651, Yazdagird III (r. 633–651), the last Sassanian king, was killed. The Arabs continued to invade land that had once been under Persian control. They took over Afghanistan and finally reached India in the early 700s. With the rise of this new Arab Islamic Empire, the last Persian Empire was gone.

PART·II

SOCIETY AND CULTURE

POLITICS AND SOCIETY IN THE PERSIAN EMPIRES

LIVING AND WORKING IN THE PERSIAN EMPIRES

PERSIAN ART, SCIENCE, AND CULTURE

CHAPTER 4

POLITICS AND SOCIETY IN THE PERSIAN EMPIRES

WITH PERSIA'S THREE DISTINCT RULING DYNASTIES stretching out over so many centuries, it is difficult to talk about one particular society or form of government. But some features do appear in all three dynasties.

All of the Persian kings were supreme rulers, although they relied on nobles for advice. In later times, the nobles played a larger role because they sometimes chose the kings. In the distant provinces of the empire, local rulers had some freedom to run their own affairs, but they would be punished for obvious disloyalty.

Women, at least in the royal families, played a greater role in society than women in most other cultures of the time did. And in the small villages and towns of the empire, the affairs of the rulers rarely touched people's daily lives—except during times of war. These Persians simply farmed or made goods, trying to live as best they could on small incomes.

THE ACHAEMENID KINGS

When the first Persian Empire arose the Near East was dominated by kings. Some ruled cities and the surrounding areas, as Cyrus the Great did in Anshan. These kings usually owed loyalty to more powerful kings. The stronger kings sometimes collected tribute from neighboring lands and they expected military help from the lesser kings when they asked for it.

None of the earlier empires in the Near East matched the size of the one built by Cyrus and his successors. The Achaemenid kings had

IN THEIR OWN WORDS

How a King Behaves

In this inscription found at Behistun, Darius described how he ruled, suggesting a model for other kings to follow.

I am of such a sort that I am a friend to right, I am not a friend to wrong. It is not my desire that the weak man should have wrong done to him by the mighty; nor is it my desire that the mighty should have wrong done to him by the weak.

What is right, that is my desire. I am not a friend to the man who is a follower of lies. I am not hot-tempered. What things develop in my anger, I hold firmly under control by my own thinking. I am firmly ruling over my own [impulses]. . . .

It is not my desire that a man should do harm; nor indeed is that my desire, if he should do harm he should not be punished. . . .

Despite what he says in this inscription, Darius had the power to kill those he thought had done harm. Herodotus recorded that Darius ordered the death of several people the king thought had disobeyed him or challenged his rule.

(Source: Wiesehofer, Josef. *Ancient Persia: From 550 BC to 650 AD*, New edition. London: I. B. Tauris, 2007.)

complete power over the lands they ruled. They made and carried out the laws and directed the military.

The kings claimed this absolute control because they believed they were chosen by the god Ahura Mazda to rule Persia and other lands. In this, the Persians followed a long tradition in the Near East—earlier kings also said they were chosen by gods to rule. Given the kings' special relationship with Ahura Mazda, disobeying them was not only a crime, it was a sin against the supreme god.

Kingship was not automatically passed from father to son. The ruling king chose his successor while he was still alive. This was often, but not always, the oldest son. The Achaemenids had several wives, primarily so they could make sure they had sons who reached adulthood and were worthy to serve as king. However, princes and others who were close to the royal family might kill chosen successors so they or someone they supported could take the throne.

When one king died, his successor's first job was to oversee the funeral. During a king's reign, a sacred fire burned at temples. The flames represented God's blessing for the king. When a king died, the fires were put out. Then new fires were lit in honor of the new king. The new king's duty was to show his military skill, live a moral life (a life in which one chooses to act correctly), and make sure his people were treated well.

LIFE AT COURT

The relatives and descendants of the six men who helped Darius gain power formed the Persian nobility (the upper class of society). These nobles could see the Great King almost any time, unless he was alone with one of his wives. They also acted as his advisors. Some nobles served as court judges, deciding cases brought to the king. However, the king could overrule their decisions.

The nobles probably wore special clothing or jewelry so others could easily identify them. Even on long marches and in battle, the Persian nobles wore their finest robes and jewelry. The wives of the Achaemenid kings were usually chosen from among the daughters of these nobles. Sons of noble families gained influence by marrying girls from the royal family.

Two Achaemenid nobles exchange a sign of friendship.

Becoming King

After Darius, the Achaemenids had a special ceremony for crowning a new king. The successor put on clothes once worn by Cyrus the Great, ate figs, and drank sour milk. The sour milk, one historian thinks, may have been used to suggest the Persians' roots as nomads. The new king then put on a royal robe with long sleeves and took several items that represented his power. These were a special headdress, a long rod called a staff, a lotus flower, and shoes that made him appear taller than he was.

The Persians had other privileged classes known as the King's Benefactors (people who help others in some way) and the King's Friends. The king gave these titles to men or groups of men who showed particular loyalty or bravery on the battlefield. The king might give the Friends and Benefactors gifts and invite them to eat with him. For most residents of the empire, though, meeting the Great King was a rare and special occasion.

The men who earned the king's rewards were not always wealthy and powerful. Plutarch, in his *Lives*, said that King Artaxerxes made "a poor, obscure man . . . a rich and honorable person" because the man gave the king a bottle of water during a battle.

Anytime two people of different social classes met, the Persians had special greetings. A person of lower rank would bow, kneel, or fall to the floor in front of the person of higher rank. Two people of equal rank might kiss each other on the lips when meeting. If one person was just slightly higher in rank, he would offer his cheek for the other person to kiss.

The boys and young men of the Persian court were trained to be military commanders. They learned to hunt with a bow and arrow while riding a horse, since those skills would also be useful on the battlefield. They also received moral teachings about telling the truth and doing what was right.

The hunt was more than a way to educate young men. The king and the nobles used hunting as a grand social event. Hunting skills were valued almost as much as battlefield heroics. Many scenes of Persian art show the kings with the animals they killed during a hunt.

WOMEN AT THE COURT

The Persians seem to have given women a greater role at court than many other ancient peoples. Although women in the Achaemenid dynasty did not rule, they could influence the king's decisions.

The mother of the king and his main wife were the two most important women in the royal family. They could see the king whenever they wanted. They were also able to eat with him, which was a rare honor. Even at banquets, the king ate in a separate room, away from the guests.

The king's mother and the queen kept watch over the royal family. If they thought one of their relatives had been mistreated, they could ask the king to punish the offender. They could also ask the king to have mercy on a noble who might have done something wrong.

These women and other royal women also had a great deal of independence. Some noble women were educated, and their studies might include horseback riding and archery, just like the education of the young men.

They owned land and kept the money their farms produced. These lands could be far beyond the Persian homeland of Persis. Herodotus, in *The Histories*, said one city in Egypt was "especially assigned to the wife of the reigning king . . . for the provision of her shoes."

The noble women traveled without their husbands—though with servants—to visit the land they owned. They also sometimes joined their husbands' trips, even into battle. The Greek historians recount examples of these noble women being captured after the battles between Alexander the Great and Darius III in the 330s B.C.E.

The women traveled in carriages, with the queen and the king's mother riding first in the line. They brought with them furniture and fine clothes, and camels carried their food. The women who traveled with the king and his nobles also included concubines who had children with the kings even though they were not married to them.

On the left is a cylinder seal from the Achaemenid dynasty and on the right is the impression it makes. It shows a scene of the queen or possibly a goddess.

LOCAL RULE

Because the empire was so big, the Achaemenid kings had to rely on loyal governors, called satraps, to carry out imperial rule. The title came from an Old Persian word meaning "protector of the kingdom." The province they ruled was a satrapy. Some local rulers in the provinces were also called kings.

With his conquest of Babylonia, Cyrus set the pattern later kings would follow. He kept the local bureaucracy already in place and put a Persian in charge as the satrap. The satrap might be a family member or a trusted noble. He might be a general rather than a civil (not military or religious) official. Cyrus also kept the local laws and system of courts in most conquered lands.

The number of satrapies varied over time. Darius the Great created 20 satrapies across the empire. Each satrapy had to raise a certain amount of taxes or tribute for the king. This could be paid in coins or in the form of horses and other goods. The satraps also had to raise armies in their lands when the king ordered. They also settled disputes that arose within their lands.

The satraps recreated life at the king's court, though on a smaller scale. They held banquets, hunted, and gave gifts. Some passed their jobs on to their sons, as the kings did. And they relied on relatives as advisors. Their capital cities, like the kings' capitals, were centers of commerce and politics. Soldiers lived in the capitals, and food and other goods were stored there.

The exact amount of freedom they had to run the satrapy is not known. In the end, they served at the king's pleasure and could be removed at any time. Throughout Persian history, satraps often

A Foreign Satrap

A Babylonian named Belesys or Belshunu (fifth century B.C.E.) may have been the only non-Persian to serve as a satrap during the Achaemenid dynasty. He was a wealthy merchant who caught the attention of Darius II. The Great King had a Babylonian mother, which might help to explain his trust of Belesys. Or the king might have been rewarding him for his support when Darius took the throne by force around 423 B.C.E.

Belesys served in Syria, and he managed to keep his position as satrap into the reign of the next king, Artaxerxes II. He stepped down in 401 B.C.E., just before Cyrus the Younger rebelled against his brother Artaxerxes. According to Xenophon, in the *Anabasis*, Belesys had a palace in Syria "with a large and beautiful park. . . . But Cyrus devastated the park and burnt down the palace."

tried to assert their independence by rebelling. Most rebellions were crushed by the central government. But satraps who followed royal orders and guaranteed the king received his taxes were not at risk.

Along the Mediterranean coast, in Asia Minor and Phoenicia, some cities were independent of the satrapies, as long as they remained loyal to the king. And in some mountain regions, nomads remained largely independent of direct government rule.

Because the empire was so big, the Achaemenid kings had to rely on loyal governors such as this one, called satraps, to rule for them.

To defend the empire and make it easy to communicate with the satraps, the Persian kings built an impressive road system. These roads made it easier for troops and supplies to move quickly around the empire. About every 15 miles along these roads, the government built inns where government officials and ordinary travelers could rest. Warehouses that held food and supplies for troops also dotted major highways.

Travelers and goods could also travel by ship. Ships regularly ran along the empire's main rivers—the Tigris, Euphrates, and Oxus. Ships also sailed on the Persian Gulf and Mediterranean and Caspian Seas.

The Persians could communicate over long distances using fire. The fires were lit on tall towers or peaks, spaced so that each tower could be seen from the next tower. Lighting one or more fires sent a certain message, such as announcing the advancement of enemy troops.

The Persians were also said to have loud voices, and some were trained to shout messages over long distances. This method worked particularly well in the mountains, where a voice would bounce off rock walls.

THE CLASSES BELOW THE NOBLES

The Persian royal family, nobles, and satraps ran the government and commanded the military. But the empire would not have survived without the efforts of social classes beneath them. These people came from many different lands and spoke a variety of languages. In some royal documents, 31 different ethnic groups are listed.

The various peoples did not resent the Persians for conquering them, although there were some exceptions. The Persians seemed to bring order and generally let people live their lives as they had before the Persians invaded. At the time, it was also common for smaller kingdoms to be swallowed by larger ones.

The military made up one important class, with various ranks of commanders. In early times, the soldiers all served part-time. Only men who could afford to own horses could join the cavalry, which was the most fearsome part of the Persian army. Poorer men became infantry soldiers. Different ethnic groups in the empire were known for their particular skills, and they formed distinct units. These included Greek hoplites and Scythian archers. Over time, the kings also hired full-time

Persian soldiers to serve in their armies. The best of the professional soldiers received farmland.

Hired workers ran the farms of the nobles and professional soldiers. The lower classes also included bureaucrats who helped run the government, artisans, and farmers who owned small plots of land. Few ancient historians describe the life of common Persians, though some facts emerge from government records discovered in Persepolis in the 1930s.

In ancient times, almost all victors in war made slaves of their defeated enemies. The Sassanians certainly did, but the Achaemenids did not seem to rely as heavily on slaves. Although some workers were forced to build buildings or work for the Achaemenid government, they were paid for their labor. Still, some foreigners in the empire lacked the freedom to live where they wanted, since the king could send them to distant lands.

PARTHIAN RULE

Under the rule of the Greek Seleucid dynasty, the satrapies remained in place. But central power was weaker than it had been under the Achaemenids. That weakness allowed small kingdoms to emerge. This happened in Parthia, which became the center of the second Persian Empire.

The Parthian kings tried to forge links to both the Greeks and Achaemenids who came before them. Greek was used as an official language for a time, and the kings wore fancy Greek headdresses rather than a soft Persian cap. Some of the Parthian kings spoke and wrote Greek, and they enjoyed Greek art.

Yet the Parthians also followed earlier Persian traditions. For example, the king was called King of Kings, one of the titles used by Darius and his successors. Fires always burned for the king and were put out at his death. The Parthian kings also promoted the old religion of Persia, Zoroastrianism. The original holy text of the Zoroastrians, the Avesta, had been destroyed during the invasion of Alexander the Great. Now the Parthians began to collect surviving copies of these texts so they could be used again.

As in Achaemenid Persia, the Arsacid kings of Parthia relied on family members and close friends as advisors and military commanders. The noble families of the Parni, the ruling clan (group of families)

Parthian Pahlavi

The original Persian name for Parthian, *Parthava*, served as the root for the word used for the Parthian language—*Pahlavi*. This language is considered one form of Middle Persian. Middle Persian is a slightly simpler form of the language used by the Achaemenids. It was spoken in Persia through the Sassanian era. Today, some northern Iranians and Kurds still use words from Pahlavi. The last ruling dynasty of Iran, which was forced from power in 1979, also took the word Pahlavi as its family name.

Greeks and Jews in the Parthian Empire

Of the different ethnic groups in Parthian Persia, modern historian Josef Wiesehofer singles out the experiences of the Greeks and Jews. In several cities throughout the empire, the Greeks enjoyed the same cultural activities they had under the Seleucids. A Greek community in Babylon had its own theater and agora, a public market and meeting place. The Greeks also provided important services as teachers, historians, and geographers.

Jewish communities also thrived in Mesopotamia, and their leaders had good relations with the Parthians. Around 21 C.E., two young Jewish men won the support of Artabanus II and were allowed to run their own independent province in Babylonia. The Jews respected the fact that the Parthians accepted their religion and were willing to work with them.

of Parthia, made up the court of the Arsacid kings who ruled Persia for almost 500 years. The families of local rulers throughout the empire also were part of the king's court. Unlike the Achaemenids, however, the Arsacids did not have absolute power over the nobles. The nobles had the right to approve a new king or get rid of one if they disliked his rule.

Just below the nobles were the wealthy landowners who formed the aristocracy, the elite class. They were called "the Greatest" and served as the heart of the cavalry in the Parthian army. They had men who served them called retainers—they owed loyalty to the aristocrats, just as local kings did to the king.

Like the Achaemenid kings, the Parthian rulers had a close circle of nobles called the King's Friends. But the Parthians went even further in honoring their most trusted advisors. From the level of First Friend, a noble could rise to the rank of Honored Friend, and even higher still was the small group of First and Most Honored Friend.

Ancient historians left few details about life among the Parthians, but nobles and aristocrats must have trained their sons for war, as the earlier Persians had. These sons might have also learned to read and write in Pahlavi (a form of Persian), and learned at least some Greek as well.

As in Achaemenid Persia, royal women had influence and a degree of independence. The king's main wife and his mother remained the most important women at court. Following Greek tradition, the wife's name began to appear in official documents. The marriages of royal daughters and nieces were also important in sealing relationships with other rulers.

LOCAL RULE

Since the Achaemenids, the size of the satrapies and the power of the satraps had shrunk. Most satraps were local officials and not members of the royal family. The position lost the prestige it once had, and the local rulers wanted to become kings and start their own dynasties. The central Parthian government accepted this, as long as the kings continued to pay taxes and pledge their loyalty to the Great King. Some

---

IN THEIR OWN WORDS

A Letter to Susa

In 1932, a block of gray marble that was once the base of a statue was uncovered by archaeologists at Susa. In the inscription on the marble, Artabanus II overrules constitutional term limits for elected officials in Susa and confirms the re-election of the city treasurer. The years Artabanus mentions refer to the calendar used during the Parthian era. The block is now on display in the Louvre Museum in Paris.

[Since Hestiaeus the son of Asius], one of your citizens and a member of the order of "the first and chief-honored friends" and of "the bodyguards," conducted himself in the office of treasurer . . . most honorably and justly and with all incorruptibility, shrinking from [no expense] of his own when the outlay was for the good of the city; twice during his term of office when the city [had] need of an envoy [he made the journey] himself, thinking the care of his own property unimportant but the city's affairs more urgent, and sparing neither money nor trouble he devoted [himself without reserve] to the two embassies, and having managed them to the city's advantage he received the

appropriate honors, as the decree voted [by the city] in the year 330 testifies.

Since in the year 331 when need arose of a good [man he was again nominated] for the same office for the year 332, and after a long examination . . . he came forward and deposed that he was debarred by the constitution from filling the same office a second time before the lapse of three years; since the city, [knowing from experience] his good character and remembering his administration of the same office, decided to choose him treasurer, and so he was elected [for the] year 332. . . .

On the above grounds, we decide that his election was valid and that he is not to be prosecuted for having filled the same office twice without allowing an interval of three years to elapse, nor on the basis of any other royal order dealing with the subject whatsoever. . . .

(Source: "Letter from Artabanus II to Susa." Parthia.com. Available online. URL: http://www.parthia.com/artabanus2_letter.htm. Accessed July 2, 2008.)

of these kings and the governments of independent cities minted their own coins and fought their own wars.

Some Greek cities in Asia Minor had been partially independent for centuries, and their residents had democratic governments. In remote areas of the steppe and mountains, tribal chiefs also kept their power. The Parthian kings, however, did not give up all rights over the local kingdoms. In one example from the first century, Artabanus II stepped in to overturn a law that would have forced a local official out of office.

The most important duty of the lesser kings was to provide soldiers for Persia during wartime. Unlike the Achaemenids, the Parthian kings did not keep a full-time army, except for troops stationed in forts across the empire and for the kings' guards. In times of war, the Parthian ruler issued a call for soldiers, and the other kings sent the men needed. These kings turned to their local aristocrats, who then recruited more troops.

THE PARTHIAN LOWER CLASSES

Below the Parthian nobles and aristocrats were two major social classes. One class consisted of free men and women. They were

From Slave to Queen

Parthian slaves almost never won their freedom or rose in social standing. But one managed to become a queen—and a notorious figure in Persian history. Thea Musa (or Thesmusa) lived in the late first century B.C.E. or the early first century C.E. She was an Italian slave who became a concubine of King Phraates IV and had a son with him. The king was obviously impressed with her, because he made her his queen.

The Jewish historian Flavius Josephus (37–ca. 100) says Thea Musa was the one who suggested Phraates send his other sons to Rome, because she wanted her son, Phraates, to become king. Josephus, in his book *The Antiquities of the Jews*, said the queen "was able to persuade [the king] to do any thing that she said . . . it was not easy for him to contradict [go against] her command."

Some historians say Thea Musa then poisoned Phraates so that her son Phraates V could take the throne. The new king created a scandal when he married his mother.

mostly peasants who had some land of their own or worked for others. Even more important were the educated or skilled free people who worked in the cities. They included artisans, artists, traders, and doctors.

But a large portion of the lower classes consisted of serfs and slaves. Serfs were people who were attached to the land they lived on and farmed. If the land changed hands, they remained and continued to work for the new owner. Their life was not much different than that of slaves.

Roman historians suggested that serfs and slaves were used as soldiers. But modern historians are not sure, since the ancient writers used different terms, such as *slaves*, *servants*, and *retinue* to describe these men. The Roman historians agreed, however, that these soldiers were different from free men.

Roman historian Justin, in his *Epitome of the Philippic History*, said owners raised their slaves "as carefully as their own children, and teach them, with great pains, the arts of riding and shooting with the bow." But, he claimed, the owners had no right to free their slaves—as masters in the Roman Empire sometimes did.

SASSANIAN SOCIETY

The Sassanians and the Arabs who defeated them left many written records, so modern historians know more about Persian politics and society during Sassanian rule. Shapur I wanted to emphasize his ties to the Achaemenids. Just as the Achaemenids did, he suggested there was a direct connection between the Persian god Ahura Mazda and Sassanian kingship.

The Sassanians created a stronger central government than the Parthians had. They relied on close ties with Zoroastrian priests and a sense of a shared Aryan culture to do so. A council of nobles played a part in approving the succession of kings, even though a reigning king normally chose a son as his successor.

A Sassanian king, like an Achaemenid king, was technically the supreme lawgiver and commander. But in practice, the king relied more on the nobles for support than the first Persian kings did.

Even more than the Parthians, the Sassanians developed strict social groups. Four classes, called estates, included everyone in the empire. These were the priests (known as magi), the warriors, state

This silver plate shows Sassanian king Shapur II hunting deer.

officials and skilled workers (such as doctors and poets), and the lower working class of artisans, peasants, and traders.

A person's position in each estate was determined by birth. So, for example, the son of a peasant would always be a peasant. Even some government positions were passed from father to son. But one ancient Persian source, quoted in the *Encyclopedia Iranica*, says that exceptions could be made "if outstanding worthiness is observed . . . in the person, after due examination by the high priests, he shall be promoted to a higher scale, subject to the approval of the King of Kings."

The warrior class included the royal family, nobles, and major landowners. In the later years of the empire, the highest priests were also included with this class. Within the warrior class there were distinct levels. At the top were the king's sons and the local kings throughout the empire. Next were members of the king's clan, then the heads of the leading families across Persia. Finally, there were free landowners who owned smaller plots of land.

Some Parthian nobles were in the early Sassanian kings' inner circle. One respected noble served as the *eran-spahbed*, the military commander. He led the troops in war and advised the king on military matters. Later, this position was divided among four generals, who each controlled the military in one quarter of the empire.

The aristocrats of Sassanian Persia worked hard to show they had a position at the top. They spent money on fancy clothes and jewels so they could easily be identified as the special people they were. They also had certain privileges. In general, they did not have to pay taxes. Their wives also had special rights to go on hunts. Noble men were allowed the largest number of wives. A noble, however, would lose his class privilege and property if he married a woman from a lower class.

As in earlier times, the kings and their nobles spent their leisure time hunting and at banquets. Education for young nobles was more developed by this time. In addition to learning military skills, they studied Zoroastrianism and learned to read and write. Some were sent to study with professional teachers, and they might also learn law and music. One ancient source records that a certain prince also learned manners and proper forms of behavior at court. The well-schooled ways of the Sassanian court served as a model for other nobility in Asia.

As in the past, royal women had influence in the Sassanian court. The king's main wife and his mother once again had the top two roles. The king could marry both Sassanian and non-Sassanian Persians, and some kings married foreign women of high rank. He could not, however, marry foreign women captured during wars, though they might become concubines.

Persian versions of such titles as *princess* and *lady* were used for different female relatives of the king. The mother of the heir to the throne was called Mother of the King of Kings. Sassanian queens traveled with their husbands across the empire and sometimes into war, and some women at court were educated. More so than in the past, queens also appeared on coins and in reliefs carved into mountains.

RULING THE EMPIRE

The Sassanian King of Kings relied on several special advisers and officials to help him run the government. These included the *hazaruft*, who was the head of the king's bodyguards, and the *vuzorg farmadar*, the man in charge of the entire bureaucracy. Other officials kept track of the gifts the kings received and made sure ceremonies were carried out according to tradition. Scribes wrote letters for the king and documented his activities, and the head of scribes was another important position.

The Sassanian kings usually named family members to rule smaller kingdoms in the empire. This arrangement helped limit the threat of rebellion in the empire. Satraps still existed, but they usually ran cities, not entire provinces, and may have been under the power of the regional king. To further limit the satraps' power, kings divided kingdoms into smaller political units run by local officials.

Eventually, power was divided up among even more officials, creating a huge bureaucracy across Persia. In the later years of the empire, the local satraps dealt with government officials called *amargars*, who handled tax affairs over a large region. Another official managed the king's various lands. A satrap or lesser kingdom also had a head magus (priest), with others below him. One special position in the provinces

Ruling Queens

In the long history of the Persian Empire, only two daughters of a king ever took the throne. During the last chaotic decades of Sassanian rule, no sons of Khosrow II were alive to take his place. Several men with loose ties to the dynasty briefly held the throne. But then the Persian nobles chose Khosrow's daughter Puran to rule. She came to power in the spring of 630. Details of her rule are scarce, but she seems to have sent diplomats to Byzantium to try to improve relations with Persia's long-time foe. Puran's reign lasted a little more than a year; she was strangled by a Persian general. Her sister Azarmigdukht briefly served after her, but almost nothing is known about her and her reign.

was created by Khosrow I. This person was the "protector of the poor and judge" who served the interests of peasants if they faced a legal trial.

THE LOWER SASSANIAN CLASSES

Below the Sassanian upper classes were various people who made their living working for others. Most farmed the land of the aristocrats, while others worked as artisans. Some fought as infantry soldiers in the army. Many of the lowest foot soldiers worked for no pay.

By the time of Khosrow I, most farmers worked for others, and the land-owning aristocrats had built tremendous political power. Khosrow created a new class of landowners, with smaller holdings, to try to reduce the power of those aristocrats.

The man in a working-class household usually had just one wife. Lower-class women of the Sassanian era were considered property and had few legal rights. They could not give evidence in court, although a woman who was not married or was under her father's care could.

A man could also give his wife to another man for a period of time, a form of marriage in Zoroastrianism called *sturih*. The wife could not refuse to go with the other man, and any children from that union were considered the children of the original husband. In this way, a man who could not have children of his own could claim to be the parent of another man's sons.

SASSANIAN SLAVERY

In hard times, a father might sell a child into slavery. Some people also became slaves for set periods of time to repay a family debt. Most slaves, however, as in the past, came from foreign conquests. The number of laws on slavery from Sassanian times suggest the practice was more developed and common than under the Achaemenids and the Parthians.

Surviving Sassanian texts have many different words for slaves, which makes it hard for modern historians to know their exact social position. A *bandag* was a person bound to another, but this could have a general meaning besides a slave. Technically, every Persian, even the great nobles, was "bound" to the King of Kings and was supposed to do his wishes.

An *ansahrig* was a foreign slave. Another term referred to a slave who worked at the fire temples used in Zoroastrianism. Some of these workers were actual slaves, who were forced to work on temple grounds. But slaves called *aduran-bandag* were free men who were bound in a symbolic way. Because of their faith, they committed themselves to helping at the temples.

At certain points during the Sassanian era, any child of a slave woman was also considered a slave. However, some writings suggest a child with a free father and slave mother would be free. Sassanian law considered slaves to be their owners' property. Yet in some cases the law does consider the slave to be a person with some legal rights, such as appearing as a witness or suing others in court. This allowed slaves to sue masters who mistreated them.

A person could also be a partial slave and keep a percentage of any money he or she earned. Some slaves used these earnings to buy their complete freedom. Slaves who practiced Zoroastrianism had special rights. They could not be sold to someone who did not follow that faith. Slaves who bought their freedom or received it from their masters became subjects of the king and apparently could not be enslaved again.

CHAPTER 5

LIVING AND WORKING IN THE PERSIAN EMPIRES

THE INSCRIPTIONS LEFT BY THE PERSIAN KINGS AND THE works of the Greek and Roman historians present a narrow slice of life in the Persian Empire. They describe the thoughts and actions of the rulers and their great battles with foreigners. But for typical subjects of the Great Kings of Persia, daily life was focused on caring for their families, raising livestock, growing crops, making and selling goods, and serving in the king's army.

Religion was also an important daily concern. Persians believed that Ahura Mazda directly influenced events on Earth.

LIFE ON THE FARM

In *The Histories*, Herodotus said that Babylonia supplied enough food to the Great King and his armies to feed them for four months of the year, and the remainder of his Asian lands supplied them for the other eight months. That meant a large amount of energy went into farming. Across the empire, some people worked for the kings and nobles, farming the fields of the rich. Others owned small plots of land. Some farmers rented plots from the richer landowners. On the steppe, nomadic herders raised livestock and traveled with their flocks as they searched for food.

Under the Achaemenids, one group of farm workers was the *kurtash*. They worked for the state, and were mostly foreign people from lands Persia conquered. The *kurtash* were not slaves, but they had

OPPOSITE

This beautiful silver and gold vase handle from the Achaemenid dynasty shows a winged ibex, a kind of wild goat.

The Persepolis Fortification Tablets

More than 2,500 years ago, Persian officials wrote in cuneiform on clay tablets to record the details of government business. During the 1930s, two sets of the tablets were found in the ruins of Persepolis. The largest group, about 30,000 tablets, is called the Persepolis Fortification Tablets.

Archaeologists have translated several thousands of the tablets, and the translations continue today. The tablets provide new details about life in Achaemenid Persia.

In recent years, they have also become tangled in a legal dispute. American survivors of a 1997 terrorist attack in Israel, along with relatives of some victims, sued the government of Iran. They claimed the Iranian government helped the terrorists. The tablets are currently at the University of Chicago, and a U.S. court ruled that they should be sold to pay the legal settlement.

The Persepolis Fortification Tablets are currently at the University of Chicago's Oriental Institute on loan from the Iranian government. The tablets are still being translated, and provide new details about life in Achaemenid Persia.

The Iranian government protested this decision, as did archaeologists who wanted to keep studying the tablets. As of early 2009, the matter was still in the courts.

to do what the government told them to. They were paid for their work, and some worked as artisans as well as farm hands.

Key crops raised across the empire included barley and other grains, flax (used to make linen), nuts, and a wide range of vegetables. Common fruits included dates, figs, plums, apples, citrus fruits, and pomegranates. Grapes were grown for wine, and barley was used for beer and bread. Cattle, goat, and sheep were raised for meat, and cattle in particular were considered a sign of wealth. The common people rarely had much meat to eat, especially in the conquered lands.

On their farms, the Achaemenid Persians dug underground canals to help irrigate (bring water to) their crops. These *qanats*, as they are called in Arabic, carried water from underground wells to fields, sometimes over long distances.

Food grown for the king was not used only to feed his family and the army. The government also gave livestock, grains, and wine as payment to various state workers. The Persepolis Fortification Tablets, a group of government records, list the rations (portions of food and drink) given to these workers. One selection from 501 B.C.E. noted, "130 liters of barley from the possessions of Amavrta have been received by Barîk-'El as his rations. Given in the town of Ithema, in the twenty-first year [of Darius] in the month Shibar."

Few details exist about farming during Parthian rule, though rice seems to have been grown for the first time in parts of the empire. Through the Sassanian period, agriculture remained a way of life for most residents of the empire. Taxes from farming provided a good deal of the king's money. The Persian historian Tabari (838–923), quoted by Josef Wiesehofer in *The Persians*, said the Sassanian king Khosrow I taxed "on the field-produce which feeds man and animal, namely wheat, barley, rice, grapes, alfalfa, date palms, and olive trees." Some

IN THEIR OWN WORDS

A Farmer's Greatest Fear

Drought (a long period without rain) is the greatest danger farmers face, even today. Persian historian Tabari described a terrible drought that hit Sassanian Persia during the mid-to-late fifth century C.E.

> *Streams, qanats, and springs dried up; trees and reed beds became desiccated [dry]; the major parts of all tillage . . . and vegetation were reduced to dust in the plains and the mountains . . . alike; bringing about the deaths there of birds and wild beasts; cattle and horses grew so hungry that they could hardly draw any loads, and the water in the Tigris became very sparse. Death, hunger, hardship . . . became general for the people of the land.*

Tillage means land used to grow crops. Tabari added that King Peroz tried to help his people get through the tough times by not collecting taxes. He also gave them permission to do whatever they needed to find food and survive the drought.

———————————

(Source: Brosius, Maria. *The Persians*. London: Routledge, 2006.)

foods, such as sesame seeds and vegetables, were not taxed, since the farmers raised them for their own families.

THE ACHAEMENID ECONOMY

The kings of Persia relied on skilled artisans to make goods for them and their armies. Merchants also played a role in the economy, buying and selling goods overseas and within the empire. Overseeing the creation and movement of many goods were various bureaucrats. Persian records, once again, offer few details about these people. But there is some information about the activities of artisans and merchants.

Under the Achaemenids, government workers called *kurtash* worked both unskilled and skilled jobs. They helped construct government buildings in Persepolis and other Persian capitals. They also built the roads that helped soldiers and goods move around the empire. The most skilled *kurtash* made goods and jewelry out of gold and silver.

The Persepolis Fortification Tablets show that skilled workers received the highest rations of food. At times they also received silver coins. The *kurtash* included women and children. Women sometimes led groups of other women in carrying out their various duties.

Jobs in the empire included making weapons, armor, and a variety of tools for farming or construction. Artisans also made vases, mirrors, and other items that were traded across the empire. Some Persians worked at the kings' huge warehouses, where supplies and food were stored for soldiers. The empire also had small factories that produced dishes and other goods for the royal family.

A large number of people worked for the king and attended to his rich

Skilled craftsmen worked for the king and supported his lifestyle. This is a golden sword from the Achaemenid period. Such a sword would not be useful in battle, but it did show off the king's wealth.

lifestyle. Greek records show that while traveling to fight Alexander the Great, Darius III had almost 300 cooks, more than 300 musicians, and 70 people whose job was to filter wine. Heraclides (fourth century B.C.E.), a Greek writer (quoted by Pierre Briant in *From Cyrus to Alexander*), described how the Great King's waiters prepared to serve him: "They . . . first bathe themselves and then serve in white clothes, and spend nearly half the day on preparations for the dinner."

Some jobs in trade and manufacturing were not tied to the government. Banking was carried out privately, and some craftsmen made goods that they traded for food or other items with their neighbors. Herodotus claimed the Persians did not have open-air markets, as the Greeks did.

In Babylonia, banking had deep roots even before it came under Persian rule. Records uncovered in the city of Nippur describe one successful family during the reign of the Achaemenids. The founder of the Murashu family was born about 500 B.C.E., and he, his sons, and grandsons made a fortune as bankers. They loaned silver coins to local residents so they could pay taxes to the Great Kings. The taxpayers repaid the loans with interest—a fee paid for the right to borrow money. One of the family's documents outlines a business deal one of the Murashu sons made. He agreed to lease farmland for 60 years, paying the owner in dates. The Murashu son would then be able to sell any other crops produced on the land.

Merchants moved a variety of goods within the empire. Many of these traders were Babylonian, since they were centrally located. Workers in Asia Minor mined iron, copper, tin, and silver. From Egypt came gold and ivory, while Phoenician winemakers provided the Persians with wine. Foreign trade went on with India and Greece. Gold from distant Siberia, in what is now Russia, seems to have reached Persia.

Buying and selling goods, especially overseas, became easier with the silver and gold coins Darius introduced. He also set up a standard system of weights and measures, so people always knew the exact amount of the goods they bought and sold.

COMMERCE IN THE LATER PERIODS

The details of economic life under the Parthians are mostly a mystery, because so few records survive. A Chinese government report on Persia from the second century B.C.E. gives one of the few descriptions of

Resource from the Earth

Even before the rise of the Achaemenids, people of the Near East knew oil was locked deep in the rocks under their lands. Some of the oil naturally oozed up to the surface, creating what are called seeps. Oil from the seeps was used in lamps, and fires at the seeps may have inspired the use of eternal fires in Zoroastrianism. Oil was most likely traded across Asia. Today, Iran and other nations once under Persian rule provide much of the oil used to make gasoline for cars and other products.

Merchants traveling the Silk Road traded goods from China to Europe. The Silk Road went through Persia, and its trade was important to the Persian economy during the Sassanian dynasty. This Chinese porcelain camel is carrying a Sassanian mask on its back, showing how cultural influences mixed along the Silk Road.

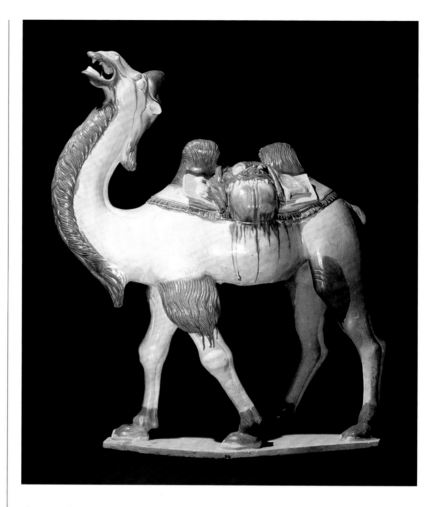

the Parthian economy. The report noted that Persia was mostly agricultural, but that "merchants . . . travel by cart or boat to neighboring states" (quoted by Maria Brosius in *The Persians*).

A major source of wealth for Persia during Parthian rule was the trade carried out along the Silk Road. This trade route was actually a series of roads that crossed Central Asia and China. Some trade was also carried out by sea. Silk, a smooth cloth spun by silkworms, was made only in China until 551. Demand for this rare cloth in Rome and Persia led to trade between the Persians and the Chinese. The Chinese sent silk, salts, and other goods to Persia.

Indian merchants also sent goods along the Silk Road through Persia, particularly spices and gems. The Persians kept some of the goods that traveled along the route for themselves and traded the rest with Rome. They also sent Rome products from Persia, such as textiles (cloth and items made from cloth). Roman goods, such as wine, glass, and wool, went through Persia back to China. The Persians also sent the Chinese horses, food, and woolen goods.

The Silk Road remained an important part of the Persian economy during Sassanian rule. Most people, however, still farmed for a living. Skilled craftsmen continued to make goods for the king. Some of them came from other countries, because the Sassanian kings sometimes took artisans from conquered or subject lands and moved them into Persia. Other such prisoners of war and their families worked in such trades as construction and blacksmithing.

FAMILY LIFE

Persian women often worked side by side with men on the farms and in workshops. And in some cases, women served as the boss of male workers. But, as in many ancient societies, family life was usually controlled by men.

The most detailed accounts of the legal dominance of men come from Sassanian times. But the importance of the father within the family and the desire to have sons go back to the earliest days of the empire. Herodotus wrote in *The Histories* that the Achaemenids believed "the goodness of a man is most signified in this: that he can show a multitude of sons. To him who can show the most, the King sends gifts every year." Many sons meant many soldiers, and also descendants to carry on the family's name.

The Sassanian records say that the husband was master of the home. By law, his wife and children had to show him

CONNECTIONS

Happy Navruz!

The ancient Persian celebration Navruz marks the new year. Navruz began on the first day of spring and lasted for several days. The celebration was first held during the Achaemenid dynasty. It took on great religious importance under the Sassanians, when it stretched out over three weeks. Although it is rooted in Zoroastrianism, over time Navruz was celebrated by Persians of all faiths.

The holiday is still observed in Iran and other lands once ruled by Persia, such as Afghanistan. It usually falls in March. In Iran, Navruz has special importance for families. Children pay respect to older relatives, and family members exchange gifts. People also visit relatives to wish them well for the new year.

proper respect. In return, the husband had specific duties. He had to support his wife for her entire life. In special circumstances, if a husband did not provide his wife with food and she was forced to steal food for survival, he was punished. If the husband died, a person chosen as guardian took care of the wife and children. The guardian was usually an adult son or another male relative, though someone outside the family could take this role.

The father was responsible for his daughters' well-being until they married, and for his sons until they became adults. In most cases, a father also had to approve a daughter's marriage partner. Daughters might marry as young as nine years old. Adult daughters had more freedom to marry whom they chose.

A household might have several generations of a family living together. Several related households, perhaps a dozen or more, formed clans. The clans shared some property and held ceremonies to honor their dead ancestors. The male leaders of the clan formed a council that watched over the weddings of clan members and heard legal disputes.

For the earlier periods of Persian history, few records exist about daily life outside the royal family. The Persepolis Fortification Tablets show that children worked for the state and received food rations, just as adults did, although the children typically received less. Mothers collected extra rations after they had children, with an added bonus if the baby was a boy. Herodotus said that boys stayed with their mothers and female relatives until they were five years old. Then they went out with their fathers to learn work skills.

EDUCATION

For the children of farmers, shepherds, and other people of the lower classes, formal schooling was rare. Children learned skills from their families. Nobles and high-ranking government officials made sure their sons could read and write. A few girls received similar lessons, but education for girls was rare. Sons of the nobility also learned how to ride horses, to hunt, and to fight.

Scribes played an important role in ancient governments, and Babylonia and Egypt set up schools to train them. Ancient sources show that when the Achaemenids conquered those lands, they kept the schools in place. Young boys studying to be scribes learned how to read and write cuneiform and also studied mathematics and astronomy. In

Babylonia, boys from lower-class jobs could enter the scribe schools. The Egyptians, however, may have limited formal education to the sons of noble families.

The Parthians did not leave records on their education system, but the average person probably could not read and write. By Sassanian times, some merchants might have learned these skills, but formal education was still rare beyond the upper classes. The importance of Zoroastrianism under the Sassanians meant students recited religious texts, and priests had to undergo years of study. Under Sassanian law, a father was supposed to make sure his children and slaves learned about Zoroastrianism. By this time, some women were also being educated outside the home.

FOOD, CLOTHING, AND SHELTER

With the variety of foods grown across the Persian Empire, the people rarely went hungry, except during droughts. For the average person, grains, beans, fruits, and vegetables were important parts of the daily diet. Beer and wine were common drinks. Spices such as coriander, basil, mint, and turmeric added flavor to many stews and other dishes.

Dried fruits and nuts were eaten throughout the empire, since they could be shipped long distances without spoiling. Other fruits and vegetables were mostly found close to where they were grown. The Persians were also the first to grow spinach, a common vegetable now found throughout the world.

The nomads of the steppe made cheese and yogurt from sheep's milk. Milk also came from goats, cattle, and horses. Meat typically came from these animals, as well as chickens and pigs. With the popularity of hunting, the nobility also ate wild game, such as wild boars, rabbits, and deer. Along the Caspian Sea, fish provided a good source of protein.

Few people ate meat regularly, but the nobles and royals did. Herodotus noted that

CONNECTIONS

A Special Belt

For ancient Zoroastrians, a white cloth belt called a *kusti* was a symbol of their faith. It was made of 72 very thin threads of wool. During the Sassanian dynasty, when boys turned 15 they received the belt as part of a ceremony that marked their becoming adults. Today's Zoroastrians still award the belt to boys and girls when they turn 15, after they demonstrate that they know the teachings of their religion.

Underground Living

In 2004, archaeologists found an underground city near the town of Noush Abad in central Iran. Parts of the city are three stories tall. The structures feature a series of halls and rooms. Some pottery at the site dates from the Sassanian period, and scholars think the underground "city" was actually a giant shelter used to protect nearby villagers. Noush Abad sits along a major trade route, so the area was often visited by robbers and foreign invaders.

birthdays were celebrated with huge feasts, with the rich serving "an ox or a horse or a camel or an ass [donkey] roasted whole in great ovens." The poor, he added, served "the smaller beasts."

Clothing differed around the empire, as various peoples wore the clothes that were common to their region. Fashions changed over time, as well. Under the Achaemenids, in Mesopotamia and North Africa, people tended to wear long gowns that reached to the ankles. In Asia Minor, shorter gowns called tunics were more common.

The Persians themselves wore a variety of garments. In works of art, Darius was shown on the battlefield in a vest, while Greek historians mentioned that the royal family wore long robes. Men also wore leather pants.

Xenophon, in his *Anabasis*, says some of the noble soldiers he traveled with wore "outer robes of purple" over "expensive tunics and colorful trousers." Purple was most often worn by the wealthy, since the dye that turned cloth purple was expensive. Few descriptions of women's dress survive, though they seem to have worn long robes and dresses. For both men and women, footwear was leather shoes or boots.

The Greeks were struck by the different types of headgear worn by the Persians and the various peoples they ruled. Hats not only kept a person's head warm and dry, they could be a sign of social rank and add color and style to a person's dress. Kings, satraps, and some nobility wore different kinds of crowns or decorated ribbons called diadems. More common were felt caps and hoods.

Under the Parthians, pants and coats with sleeves similar to modern clothing became common across the empire. Both men and women, however, still sometimes wore tunics. Tunics were also worn during the Sassanian era, with men wearing shorter tunics and trousers. Royalty sometimes tied long ribbons around their pants at the ankles. In the later years of the Sassanian Empire, kings and other royalty also wore long robes.

All the Persians wore belts, either tied or buckled. During the Parthian and Sassanian dynasties, belts were more commonly worn by men.

Written records and art provide good information on Persian clothing, but there is less information on housing. In ancient times, before the Achaemenids, some Persians lived in caves. In the Sassanian era, people sometimes dug underground shelters, as recent archaeological discoveries have shown. Nomads lived in tents, which could be quickly set up and taken down.

The kings of Persia built tremendous stone and brick palaces. Smaller homes for common people were usually made out of mud bricks. When traveling, the kings set up huge tents to hold all their relatives, aides, and supplies.

THE ROLE OF RELIGION

Before the rise of the Achaemenids, the people of Media and Persis worshipped many gods. Even Darius, who praised Ahura Mazda as the greatest of the gods, acknowledged others. But over the centuries, Ahura Mazda, which means "Wise Lord," became the primary god for many Persians. Their religion, Zoroastrianism, centered on the worship of him.

The roots of the religion are traced to a prophet (a person who claims to speak for a god) called Zarathustra by the Persians and Zoroaster by the Greeks. The prophet received visions from the god Ahura Mazda and convinced a legendary Persian king named Vishtap to worship this god. Zoroaster said that Ahura Mazda was supreme over all the other gods the Persians worshipped. He then set down the first teachings of the religion in writings called the Gathas.

IN THEIR OWN WORDS

The Zoroastrian Creed

A creed is a statement of the basic ideas accepted by the followers of a particular religion. For Zoroastrians, their creed appears in the 12th part of the *Yasna*, which is one section of the Avesta. The creed is thought to have been written by Zoroaster and repeated by the people he converted to the new faith. Here is a small part of it.

I reject the authority of the Daevas [false gods], the wicked, no-good, lawless, evil-knowing . . . the foulest of beings, the most damaging of beings. I reject the Daevas and their comrades, I reject the demons (yatu) and their comrades; I
reject any who harm beings. I reject them with my thoughts, words, and deeds. I reject them publicly. . . .

I profess myself a Mazda-worshipper, a Zoroastrian, having vowed it and professed it. I pledge myself to the well-thought thought, I pledge myself to the well-spoken word, I pledge myself to the well-done action.

———————

(Source: "Yasna 12—The Zoroastrian Creed." Translated by Joseph H. Peterson. Avesta–Zoroastrian Archives. Available online. URL: http://www.avesta.org/yasna/y12j.htm. Accessed May 3. 2008.)

Fire altars used by Zoroastrian priests at the tomb complex of the Sassanian kings at Naqsh-e Rostam.

Historians are not sure when Zoroaster lived. Some argue it was around 1200 or 1000 B.C.E., while others say the seventh century B.C.E. is more likely. He lived in what is now eastern Iran or western Afghanistan. There are few details of his life, except for what is in the Gathas. At first he had trouble winning over followers, but by the time of the Achaemenids his religion had spread across Persia.

The holy books of Zoroastrianism, the Avesta, contains the Gathas and later teachings of the religion. For centuries, the Avesta was passed on orally, though some written pieces also existed. Historians think the first complete written version appeared under the Sassanians, around the fourth century C.E.

The core of Zoroastrian beliefs is that forces of good and evil constantly battle each other. Humans must choose which force they will support. Ahura Mazda represents the force of good—particularly truth, order, and moral action—while a god named Ahriman represents evil. Demons do his work on Earth. Zoroastrians believe that after they die, they will face a day of judgment and be sent to either heaven or hell, depending on whether they had sided with Ahura Mazda or supported the forces of evil during their life.

Sacred fires were lit at temples to honor Ahura Mazda, and priests carried out the rituals (religious ceremonies) of worship. These included offering sacrifices—animals killed or valuables offered—to show respect and ask for the god's help.

Historians think Zoroastrian ideas may have influenced Jewish and Christian beliefs. And, like Judaism and Christianity, modern Zoroastrianism is considered a monotheistic religion—only one god is worshipped.

Zoroastrianism was not always completely monotheistic, though. The Achaemenids considered Ahura Mazda to be the supreme god, but under them the Persians also worshipped Mithra, the sun god, and Anahita, who was the goddess of water and fertility (the ability to produce offspring). And while the sun, moon, and natural elements (water, sky, earth, fire) were not gods, they were considered holy. Herodotus said in *The Histories* that the Persians "revered rivers most of all things" and would not wash their hand in them or let others do so. Records from Persepolis show the Persians used wine as a sacrifice to the rivers as well as to gods.

CONNECTIONS

A Magical Word

The word for a Zoroastrian priest is *magus*. It comes from a Persian word meaning "sorcerer" (a wizard or magician), although some sources say it means "great one." The plural is *magi*. The Greek form of the word served as the root for the English word *magic.*

The first magi were members of a Medean tribe who served as priests for the Zoroastrian religion. In Christianity, the three wise men who visited the baby Jesus were called the magi, though there is no hard evidence that they came from Persia or practiced Zoroastrianism.

The Zoroastrians did not believe in burying bodies in the ground. The earth was considered holy, and they did not want to pollute it with dead flesh, which was thought to be filled with evil spirits. Herodotus described how Zoroastrian magi let dogs or birds eat at the flesh. The remaining bones were then placed in a deep well or other spot underground. This practice was most common in the western parts of the Persian Empire.

Under the Achaemenids, Zoroastrianism seems to have been practiced mostly by the royal family and the nobility. Some of the kings rode into battle with an empty chariot beside them, pulled by white horses. The chariot was said to belong to Ahura Mazda, who would watch over the Great Kings as they fought.

The average Persians still worshipped old gods that dated from before Zoroaster. The non-Persian people of the empire were free to worship their local gods. The Persian kings knew they could win the support of conquered people by offering this freedom and by claiming they acted in the local gods' name. Darius the Great, for example, left an inscription in Egypt that called the god Amun-Re his father.

But the Persians were less tolerant if one of their foreign peoples rebelled. Around the 480s B.C.E., Xerxes either destroyed or threatened to destroy a temple in a land where his rule had been challenged.

In *The Histories*, Herodotus offered one view of early Zoroastrian practices and beliefs. He said that Persians, unlike the Greeks, did not give their gods human form, and they did not worship in temples. When a person wanted to make a sacrifice, "He brings into an open space his sacrificial beast and calls upon the god. . . . He may pray not for good things for himself alone . . . but only that all shall be well with all the Persians and the king. . . ." Since the Persians did not depict Ahura Mazda as human, his presence is shown in art through the image of a winged disc.

RELIGION UNDER THE PARTHIANS AND SASSANIANS

The Parthians kept up the old practice of allowing the worship of many gods across the empire. Although the rulers believed in Ahura Mazda, they also accepted other gods. Zoroastrianism seemed to decline for several centuries. King Vologeses, who ruled during the middle of the first century, tried to strengthen Zoroastrian beliefs and practices. Coins printed during his reign showed the sacred fires that always burned for Ahura Mazda. He is also said to have tried to collect together various hymns and religious writings.

A stronger revival of Zoroastrianism came under the Sassanians. The kings and nobles embraced it, and more fire altars appeared. The number of magi grew, and some seemed to have great influence over certain kings. At times, these magi used this power to try to stamp out other religions. But although Zoroastrianism was the state religion it existed side by side with the other faiths of the empire. During the Sassanian era, these included Buddhism and Christianity. Buddhism had developed in India in the sixth century B.C.E., and then spread to other parts of Asia. Christianity developed in what is now Israel.

Another new religion during the Sassanian era had its roots in Persia. During the third century, a Babylonian named Mani (ca. 216–ca. 276) began blending Jewish, Christian, Buddhist, and Zoroastrian beliefs. Mani said that everything in the universe came from a mixture of light and darkness, in which light stood for peace and darkness stood for conflict. The world of light was the spiritual world, while life

Zoroaster in Art

Zoroaster's name is well known today in its Persian form, Zarathustra, thanks to two works of art. In 1896, the German writer Friedrich Nietzsche wrote a book titled *Also Sprach Zarathustra (Thus Spoke Zarathustra)*. Nietzsche used the Persian prophet as a character in a long poem that explained Nietzsche's ideas about life. Those ideas had nothing to do with Zoroastrianism. A German composer, Richard Strauss, then wrote a piece of music using the same title.

Nietzsche's book is studied in schools around the world and Strauss's music is still played by orchestras. It also became very famous as the theme music for the movie *2001: A Space Odyssey*. Zoroaster's writings, however, are barely known except to scholars and followers of his faith.

on Earth was the world of darkness. By living well, people could begin to separate the light and darkness within them. His religion was called Manichaeanism. There was no one supreme god, as in the monotheistic religions.

Mani traveled throughout the Persian Empire spreading his new religion. The king at the time, Shapur I, did not follow the new faith, but he let Mani teach it and some members of the royal family became followers. Mani claimed his teachings came from an angel and would last longer than any other known religions.

Zoroastrian priests rejected Mani and his teachings, and they convinced a later Persian king to have Mani arrested. His religion, though, continued to grow, eventually spreading west into the Roman Empire and east into China.

Another new religion that developed during the Sassanian Era was Mazdakism. Its founder, Mazdak, stirred social and political conflict with his teachings. He seemed to borrow some ideas from both Manichaeanism and Zoroastrianism. Mazdak and his beliefs briefly had some government support. But then the Sassanians turned against them and tried to stamp out the new faith. Some followers, however, lived in Persia until the end of the empire.

JUDAISM IN PERSIA

When the Medes and Persians were emerging as powers in Mesopotamia, the Jews had already built a great kingdom and then seen it fall under enemy attacks. Their religion, Judaism, was the first major monotheistic religion in the ancient world. The Jewish homeland, Israel, was located along the Mediterranean Sea and was centered in what is now the modern nation of Israel.

The original Israel split into two kingdoms during the 10th century B.C.E. During the eighth century B.C.E., the Assyrians asserted their power in the region. The Assyrians and after them the Babylonians sent many Jews to live in Mesopotamia.

Cyrus the Great was a hero to the Jews, because he freed them from Babylonian rule and helped them rebuild their temple in Jerusalem. Under the various Persian rulers, Israel was sometimes under direct Persian control, and many Jews lived throughout the empire. The Jews were mostly allowed to live as they chose.

CONNECTIONS

Iranian Jews Today

The Jewish community in Iran is more than 2,500 years old. During the centuries after the end of the Sassanian Empire, many Jews left the country or were forced to convert to Islam. Still, today 25,000 remain. They are the largest Jewish population in the Middle East outside of Israel.

During the early 2000s, Iran's president made harsh remarks about Israel and the suffering of millions of Jews in Europe during World War II. Still, most of the remaining Jews in Iran do not feel threatened and are proud of their deep roots in the country. In 2007, one leading Jewish resident of Tehran told the *Christian Science Monitor*, a U.S. newspaper, "I speak in English, I pray in Hebrew, but my thinking is Persian."

Under the Persians, some Jewish soldiers served the government in Egypt. A rebellion broke out near the Jewish post in the early 400s B.C.E. An ancient letter from the Jewish troops to the local satrap (cited by E. Bresciani in the *Cambridge History of Iran*) said that during the rebellion, ". . . we did not leave our posts and no disloyalty was found in us."

Under the Parthians, the Jewish community also had good relations with the government. In Babylon, they played a part in building the silk trade with China. When Jews under Roman control faced persecution, they sometimes moved to Parthian lands, where they knew they could live as they chose. The Jews of Roman Syria welcomed Parthian troops when they invaded that region in the 160s. The Sassanians continued the tolerant treatment of the Jews.

CHRISTIANITY IN PERSIA

During the first century, a new monotheistic religion developed in Judea, the Roman province that had once been the kingdom of Israel. A Jewish man named Jesus taught about the importance of love and worshipping God to achieve life after death in heaven. Jesus won followers but also angered some Jewish leaders because some of his teachings went against Judaism.

Jesus was crucified—nailed to a cross—for his beliefs. This was a typical Roman punishment of the day. His followers, called disciples, said that he rose from his grave and thus proved he was the Son of God. These followers were the first members of the religion called Christianity.

This new faith soon spread to Persian lands. The biggest development came under the Sassanian king Shapur I. He sent thousands of Christians from Syria and Asia Minor to live in the heart of Persia. He wanted them to work for the government as artisans and construction workers. This movement of people created large Christian communities.

For several decades, the Christians lived peacefully under the Sassanians. After Rome's emperors embraced Christianity in the fourth century, Sassanian leaders feared some local Christians might be spies for the Romans. Over time, the persecutions led to some Persian Christians being killed because of their faith. Relations between the government and Christians improved slightly in 410, when the Christians created their own local church, separate from the Christian church based in the eastern half of the Roman Empire. New persecutions, however, broke out during the sixth century.

CHAPTER 6

PERSIAN ART, SCIENCE, AND CULTURE

THE PERSIANS, LIKE THE OTHER PEOPLE OF THE ANCIENT Near East, had skilled artisans who created beautiful and practical works of art. They also had architects who designed impressive buildings, and artists who carved stone reliefs. But the Persians did not leave behind the wide range of artistic achievements in writing, painting, and sculpture that the Greeks and Romans did. Few of these items have survived to today, so it is hard to know exactly what they achieved in those areas.

ACHAEMENID ART AND CULTURE

Achaemenid art ranged from the huge stone reliefs carved into mountains and royal palaces to small, carefully crafted pieces of jewelry. The stone reliefs are an important source of historical information and help us understand life at the Persian court. They often show the king victorious in battle or after a hunt or receiving gifts from visitors.

Many of the most impressive Achaemenid buildings were constructed in Persepolis and the other capitals of the empire. The Persian architects blended existing styles of columns from Greece, Egypt, and other lands with their own designs.

One local touch was carving heads of bulls or other animals on the tops of columns. Some of the figures also combined human and animal features in one beast. One bull's head atop a column at Persepolis—now on display at Chicago's Oriental Museum—weighed 10 tons. The carvings at the palaces and other royal buildings were

OPPOSITE

This is a gold rhyton, a type of drinking cup used by the Achaemenid court. The lower part usually featured an animal—in this case, a lion with wings.

CONNECTIONS

In Paradise

At their palaces, the Persian kings built enclosed grounds called *paridaida*. Inside the walls, the kings raised a wide variety of trees, plants, and flowers, with water coming from *qanats*. At times, the king also brought animals into the *paridaida* and used it as private hunting grounds. The *paridaida* gave the king a peaceful, beautiful spot to enjoy nature and relax. The lush garden was a splash of life and color in what could be the harsh climate of the desert and the steppe.

Borrowing from the Persians, the Greeks called these grounds *paradeisos*. This is the root of the English word *paradise*—a beautiful and peaceful spot.

done in stone, while the walls were usually made from mud bricks.

The building projects at Darius's capital at Persepolis were the model other Achaemenids followed. And the most impressive building there was the Apadana, the great hall. Two staircases led to the hall. On the sides were reliefs showing visitors and Persian nobles going to see the Great King. The way one relief is positioned, the stone guests appear to be walking up the stairs. The main hall of the Apadana had 36 columns. Each was more than 60 feet tall.

Other notable buildings at Persepolis included the Hall of a Hundred Columns, which could hold several thousand people. There were also several palaces.

Inside the palace at Susa, artisans used colored tiles and bricks to create designs and scenes of people. The work was skilled enough to show the folds in the robes worn by soldiers and the rippling muscles of walking lions. Darius left an inscription about his palace at Susa (quoted by Lindsay Allen in *The Persian Empire*): "At Susa a very excellent work was ordered, a very excellent work was accomplished."

The palaces of the Achaemenids are in ruins now, and only pieces of the buildings and the artwork that covered them remain. But many of the stone reliefs are still intact, showing the Persian skill with this art form. The most famous, at Behistun, is some 60 feet above the ground. The scene shows Darius the Great standing over the men he defeated to become king. The carving covers an area about 26 feet high and 59 feet long. Historians are not sure how the carvers cut the stone to create this monument, but it created a style that other Persian kings followed.

Inside their palaces, the Persian kings surrounded themselves with useful art. Using gold, silver, bronze, and clay, their artisans made bowls, utensils, and drinking cups called rhytons. With a rhyton, a cone-shaped part held the liquid, which was then drunk through a spout near the bottom. The lower part of the rhyton usually featured an animal, such as a gazelle or lion, and the spout might serve as the animal's mouth.

In Persian crafts, animals also sometimes appeared on the handles of jugs and jars used to hold wine. Items such as rhytons, utensils, and jewelry have been found in graves, and they often appear in scenes of Persian life shown on reliefs.

Animals were also shown in art as part of a favorite Persian social event—the hunt. One seal used by a king to mark his official documents showed a lion hunt, with the king using a bow and arrow while riding in a chariot. For the nobles, hunting was a way to relax, as well as sharpen the skills used in warfare.

Another important social event was the banquet. In their different palaces or in tents while they traveled, the kings hosted huge, lavish meals for the court and foreign guests. The banquets let the king show his wealth and power and keep the loyalty of the people below him. One ancient Greek historian recorded that 1,000 animals were

CONNECTIONS

Persian Rugs

Today, so-called Persian rugs or carpets are produced across Iran. The first were probably made more than 2,500 years ago by the nomads of the steppe, who placed them over the dirt floors of their tents. Other times, they wrapped themselves in the rugs to keep warm. Rug makers made threads from the wool of their sheep and goats. The woolen threads were dyed different colors, using plants and roots to make the dyes. Then they were knotted together to make carpets.

By the time of the Achaemenids, the Persians were already famous for their colorful, well-made carpets, which featured fancy designs and images of people and animals. The skill of the carpet weavers made Persian rugs valuable pieces of art.

In Iran today, weavers in certain cities are known for particular styles of rugs, which can sell for thousands of dollars. Antique Persian rugs are even more expensive.

killed every day for one Persian king's banquets, though most of the meat went to soldiers outside the palace, not the guests.

In their writings, Herodotus and Xenophon suggest that music was part of the cultural life of the Persian royalty and nobility. Musical instruments were played in Persia and neighboring lands before the rise of the Achaemenids, and included different styles of flutes and stringed instruments.

ACHAEMENID SCIENCE AND TECHNOLOGY

The ancient Persians learned from the cultures around them, borrowing ideas and at times improving on them. Astronomy, the study of the movement of the stars and planets, was blended with astrology—using the position of the planets to predict the future. The Babylonians began recording the movement of the moon and planets around 700 B.C.E., and they remained the key astronomers under Persian rule.

Tracking the movement of the sun and moon helped astronomers create calendars. The Persian calendar of the Achaemenids had 12 months, and they also used a second calendar based on Zoroastrian teachings. A later version of this Avestan calendar used the names of gods and holy items, not numbers, to mark the different days in the month.

In technology, the Persians focused on improving irrigation. These included underground water channels called *qanats*. The Achaemenids also built large dams to control the flow of water for human use. These dams were made of soil and stone and helped hold in the heavy rains that fell during certain times of the year, saving the water for irrigation.

Warfare also sparked new engineering feats. In *The Histories*, Herodotus described how Xerxes built one of the earliest known pontoon bridges. This kind of bridge uses small boats or other floating devices to hold up a roadway that carries traffic over water. Herodotus said the Persians used more than 600 boats to build two bridges. It had thick cables strung over the boats and wooden logs over the cables. Walls on the side of bridge were put up "so that the baggage animals and horses might not see the sea beneath them and take fright."

Dam Discovery

In 2007, a team of Japanese and Iranian archaeologists working in Iran announced the discovery of a soil dam dating back to Achaemenid times. Outer walls of stone covered the dam, though only part of the stonework and the soil itself still remain. Mohsen Zeidi, head of the team, described to reporters (as reported by the Cultural Heritage News Agency) how a canal 22 miles long "was constructed from the Polvar River to this dam . . . in order to direct part of the extra waters left by the seasonal flooding toward the reservoir of the dam to supply water. . . ." Soil dams of this construction are still used today in some dry areas of Iran.

Achaemenid science also included some knowledge of medicine, though the Persians of the era believed medicine was rooted in religion. The Avesta contained books on medicine, as well as other scholarly fields, supposedly written by Zoroaster himself. The Zoroastrian priests were considered the most skilled in offering cures. They used basil, peppermint, and other plants and herbs as medicine.

PARTHIAN ART AND CULTURE

By the time the Parthians emerged, Persia was increasingly influenced by Greek art and culture. That influence shows in some of the art and buildings created under Parthian rule. Greek styles and subjects often turned up in sculpture. The Greek influence weakened over the centuries, and the Parthians also drew on Persian and Near Eastern influences. Along the way, they introduced new styles and techniques.

In buildings, Parthian architects stopped using columns to support the weight of roofs. The columns were used merely as decorations. The Parthians perfected the barrel vault, a kind of domed roof that had first appeared centuries before. The Parthian version was much larger than earlier barrel vaults and was used to create the *ivan*, a hall that opened up into a courtyard. This building style later influenced the Sassanians and the Arabs.

Inside buildings, the Parthians covered the walls with stucco, a material made of cement and minerals. Artisans created patterns and images of plants and people in the stucco to decorate the walls.

The Parthians also came up with a distinct building style for military uses. Along their borders in Central Asia and Mesopotamia they built forts large

Wonders of Nisa

Some of the best examples of Parthian art and architecture were uncovered at a city that is known today as Nisa. Nisa was located in the old Parthian homeland, in what is today Turkmenistan, and was divided into Old and New Nisa. The Parthians called the city Mithradatkirt, in honor of its builder, Mithridates I.

Archaeological digs at the royal palace in Old Nisa have revealed many statues in both clay and stone that combine Greek and Parthian styles. Paintings found on the walls also combine these styles. The architecture, however, was less influenced by the Greeks and seems to reflect local styles. In 2007, the remains at Nisa were named a World Heritage Site by UNESCO.

Hatra, a trading center in southwestern Mesopotamia, has several examples of Parthian art and architecture. As this temple in Hatra shows, Parthian architects stopped using columns to support the weight of roofs. The columns were simply decorations.

enough to hold military officers, cavalry and infantry, and the peasants and artisans who supported them. One unique design set up the fort in a circle, so the defenders could more easily repel attacks from the sides. The Parthians may have used a similar circular defense when they were still nomads living on the steppe.

Another artistic change in Parthian times came in stone reliefs. For the first time, bodies were shown from the front as well as from the side. Some notable Parthian stone reliefs were carved at Behistun, just as the Achaemenids had done. One, now badly damaged, showed Mithridates II beginning his rule as king. Another featured King Gotarzes II (r. ca. 91–ca. 81 B.C.E.) after winning a joust.

Reliefs in the Parthian style also appeared in some of the kingdoms that made up the Parthian Empire. Elymais, in what is now southern Iran, had many stone reliefs. One showed a jousting noble. Elymais was also the home of perhaps the most famous piece of Parthian art, a sculpture of a prince. The bronze work stands just over six feet tall and shows the details of Parthian dress.

Hatra, a trading center in southwestern Mesopotamia, was independent of Parthian Persia, but it had many examples of Parthian art. One temple had five *ivans.* Sculpture throughout the city showed local nobility wearing Parthian clothes and hairstyles.

The statues of Hatra show that skilled artisans continued to produce dazzling examples of their craft, because personal items were clearly shown on the subjects carved in stone. Jewelry showed a person's social position, so the wealthy wore large gold items sometimes decorated with pearls. Weavers might include strips of gold and silver in the clothing they made for the wealthy. And at Nisa, archaeologists have uncovered rhytons made of ivory.

Parthian rulers and nobility were exposed to Greek writings, but the Parthians themselves relied mostly on spoken tales and poems for their literature. Legends about past heroes were mixed with stories of the Arsacid kings, and these tales were told or sung by musician-storytellers called *gosans.* One tale of love among the nobility, *Vis and Raman*, provided the source for later Persian writings.

Historians do not know much about the *gosans*, though the tales and skills needed to perform were likely passed from father to son. The *gosan* played a lute, similar to a guitar. Few ancient texts talk about other instruments played in Parthian Persia, though they probably had not changed much since Achaemenid times.

For recreation, the Parthians hunted, as the Achaemenids did. They also introduced a new,

Art in War

The Parthians and other Iranian people of the steppe crafted a useful piece of art for their military. Out of metal, they formed the head of a dragon or other beast with its mouth open wide. Behind the head streamed a long cloth sock. As the person holding the head rode forward into battle, air rushed through the dragon's mouth, filling the sock and making it wriggle. This made the dragon appear to come to life. At the same time, the wind passing through the mouth created an eerie sound meant to scare enemy troops.

The dragon head also helped indicate the direction of the wind, helping archers shoot their arrows. The Romans borrowed the idea of using these dragon heads, or *dracos*, and they appeared on European battlefields for centuries after the fall of Rome.

The wealthy people in Parthian times wore large gold items, such as this necklace.

formal type of exercise called Varzesh-e Pahlavani. Modern writers have compared it to a martial art, such as karate, that stressed a blend of physical and mental training. The athletes, called Pahlavanis, trained in a round building called a *zurkhanen*, which means "house of strength." The exercises they performed included swinging wooden clubs. These were designed to strengthen them for horse riding and boxing. As the Pahlavanis trained, a drum-

CONNECTIONS

Today's Houses of Strengths

The Parthian tradition of Varzesh-e Pahlavani survives in Iran today. Some of the athletes who train in *zurkhanens* are competitive wrestlers. Iranians are known for their wrestling skills, and many have won medals at the Olympic Games. In recent years, *zurkhanens* have also appeared in lands once ruled by Persia, such as Iraq, Tajikistan, and Afghanistan. The training centers have also opened in countries where Iranian immigrants have settled, such as Canada and Germany. In 2008, and international sporting event held in South Korea featured Varzesh-e Pahlavani athletes.

mer kept a beat and a musician sang poems. The best of the athletes from the *zurkhanens* were respected for their strength.

PARTHIAN SCIENCE AND TECHNOLOGY

Under the Parthians, Babylonia remained a center for astronomy. Some ideas about the stars and planets also began to reach Persia from Asia. In medicine, some knowledge from Greece blended with the traditional Zoroastrian teachings. Details here, though, as with other parts of Parthian life, are few.

The Parthians may have also harnessed power from the world's first crude batteries. A jar discovered near Baghdad in 1938 held a copper cylinder that surrounded an iron rod. Those two metals, when placed in certain chemicals called electrolytes, can produce electricity. Other jars like the one in Baghdad have been found, and scientists have created their own versions of the jars to show they could produce electricity using vinegar, lemon juice, or wine as the electrolyte.

The Parthians may have used their "batteries" to put a layer of gold over other metals, a process called electroplating. As one scientist told the British Broadcasting Company in 2003, "I don't think anyone can say for sure what they were used for, but they may have been batteries because they do work."

SASSANIAN ART AND CULTURE

Compared to the two Persian empires that came before them, the Sassanians left the most detailed records of their world. Muslim historians writing after the end of Sassanian rule also added to the knowledge of their art and culture.

The Sassanian kings continued the tradition of carving reliefs and inscriptions in stone. Ardashir, the first king of the dynasty, carved reliefs at Naqsh-e Rostam, where Darius and several other Achaemenid kings were buried. Ardashir clearly wanted to make a connection to the first great Persian dynasty by choosing this spot and continuing the artistic style the Achaemenids used. The Sassanians also followed Parthian traditions, using the reliefs to show scenes of kings taking power and of jousting matches.

In architecture, the Sassanians also kept some Parthian styles. Their palaces featured *ivans*, with their barrel vaults, and cities were often laid out in a circular pattern. The Sassanians perfected the use of domed ceilings. They constructed arched supports in the corners of the room, called *squinches*. The dome then rested on the *squinches*. This design was later copied and developed further in European and Arab lands.

Inside their buildings, the Sassanians covered their walls with stucco and sometimes painted it bright colors. Stucco was also used to create reliefs on walls and to make other decorations.

With their deep Zoroastrian faith, the Sassanians erected many fire temples across the empire. One of the largest was Adur Gushnasp, in what is today Takht-e Suleiman in northern Iran. One room held a fire that always burned, while another room was used for special rites. During the rule of Khosrow II, in the 620s, the temple was attacked. The Sassanians built a wall 50 feet tall and 10 feet thick to defend it against future attacks.

Sassanian artisans showed high skill in weaving, making jewelry, and glassmaking. Some of the most beautiful works of art were made in silver, including plates, bowls, and cups. Silver plates often featured reliefs that showed the king hunting or taking part in other activities. In their arts and crafts, the Sassanians often featured lions, elephants, and fantastic beasts, as well as plants, geometric shapes, and detailed patterns. Sassanian silver was prized in both Europe and China. The Chinese also copied Sassanian art patterns when printing silk clothing.

A Grand Palace

Perhaps the greatest Sassanian building was the Palace of Khosrow, near Ctesiphon. It had a huge *ivan*, 143 feet long and 84 feet wide, covered with a large arching roof. The vault was believed to be the largest ever made in Persia. The palace was already in partial ruins in 1888 when a huge flood destroyed about one-third of what was still standing.

The Sassanians did not leave behind much literature, other than the *Avesta*, which was compiled during their dynasty. The *Karnamak Ardashir*, or *Records of Ardashir*, was written around 600, and is said to be a history of the first Sassanian king. Fragments of other kings' records have also survived, and some Sassanian writings are known through later Arabic translations. Some written hymns from Manichaean religious services have been found, and the Sassanians wrote down some poems; these works did not use rhymes. The Sassanians also continued the musical and poetic tradition of the *gosan*.

Sassanian musical forms were highly developed, and Persian musicians and instruments were respected by the Chinese and the Arabs. Different forms of music were used for different events—celebrations, religious ceremonies, and military activities. Drums and gongs were used on the battlefield to send signals to troops. When he was hunting, the king was accompanied by musicians playing flutes and stringed instruments. One bowl shows an instrument similar to a bagpipe.

The Sassanians and Greeks seem to have exchanged musical ideas with each other. This was probably also true of the Romans.

CONNECTIONS

Tars, Sitars, and Guitars

In ancient Persia, one stringed instrument was the *tar*. Its name came from the Persian word for "stringed" or "hair." By the time of the Sassanians, different types of *tars* were played across the empire. They had varying number of strings. One of these, the *setar*, had three strings (*se* meaning "three") This instrument found its way to India, where it became known as the sitar.

The sitar is still played in India, although the modern version has more than three strings. During the 1960s, a master of the sitar, Ravi Shankar, played his instruments in concerts in the United States and Europe. As a result, sitar music became popular in the West. Sitars are still used in some Western music today.

The Persian *tar* also may have influenced the development of the guitar. Arabs who settled in Spain may have brought their version of the Persian stringed instruments. Another Persian stringed instrument, the *santur*, shaped the development of the hammered dulcimer, which is played in some American folk music. As the name suggests, the musician uses small sticks to hammer on the strings.

The game of chess spread from Persia to other parts of Asia and then into Europe. This chess piece shows an elephant.

One work of art in Constantinople shows a Byzantine empress welcoming Sassanian musicians to her court.

According to the *Records of Ardashir*, Ardashir I was skilled at chess and backgammon. Chess was thought to have originated in India and come to Persia, but it probably reached there after

Ardashir lived. From Persia, the game spread to other parts of Asia and then into Europe. The English word *chess* traces its roots to *shah*, the Persian word for *king*. The chess term *checkmate* comes from *shah-mat*, meaning the king (the game piece) cannot move.

SASSANIAN SCIENCE AND TECHNOLOGY

Like the Persian rulers before them, the Sassanians supported the study of the skies. And they continued the tradition of using the best scientific knowledge from other lands. Kings Ardashir I and Shapur I had astronomy and astrology books from Greece and India translated into Pahlavi, the Parthian language still in use at the time. Today astrology is not considered a science, but in ancient times it was. Sassanian scholars also studied mathematics. In the Arab era that followed, some of the best mathematicians were Persian.

In medicine, the Sassanians also borrowed from the Greeks and the Indians, while keeping alive old traditions. In the sixth century, Khosrow I sent his personal doctor, Burzoye, to India to collect medical writings. Khosrow also organized what seems to have been the first medical convention. In *The Persians*, Josef Wiesehofer cites a Christian book of laws that notes, "[T]the physicians of Jundaisabur [Gundeshapur in Iran] assembled for a scientific symposium [meeting] by order of the king. Their debates were recorded. . . . One has only to take a look at the questions and definitions discussed here to realize the extent of their knowledge and their experience."

The Avesta offered some of the most detailed descriptions of medicine during this period. The Zoroastrians recognized three kinds of doctors: those who cured with a knife (surgeons), those

CONNECTIONS

Backgammon in Persia

By some accounts, the disc-and-dice game called backgammon was created in India and then taken into Persia. Others say the game's roots were in Mesopotamia. Learning the game, called *nard* in Persian, was considered an important part of a Sassanian noble's education. One text, however, *The Councils of the Wise Osna,* says playing the game too often was bad for a man's character.

In 2004, archaeologists may have found proof that backgammon was actually invented in Persia, or was at least played there long before the rise of the first Persian dynasty. An archaeological dig in southeastern Iran uncovered a backgammon board and game pieces that were almost 5,000 years old.

The First Teaching Hospital

In Persian, a hospital was called a *bimare-stan* or "place of the sick." The Sassanians are credited with creating the first teaching hospital, where students learned medicine while also helping doctors treat patients. This first teaching hospital appeared during the reign of Ardashir I. This idea was developed even further under Khosrow I. The hospital was located at Gundeshapur, in southwest Iran, and was connected to a medical school.

During the sixth and seventh centuries, the medical center was the most important one of its kind in the world. Scholars from Greece, Persia, and India went there to study medicine. Student doctors at the hospital trained with a variety of skilled doctors. Above a door entering the medical school were the words, "Knowledge and virtue are superior to sword and strength" (quoted online at Press TV.com).

Gundeshapur remained an important medical center into the Arab era. In the 20th century, two new universities named for it opened near where the original hospital once stood.

who cured with medication, and those who used magical words and religious chants (these doctors have been compared to modern psychologists, who talk with patients to solve emotional problems). The value of herbs as medication appears in the Avesta. One section says, "Ahura Mazda brought down the healing plants that, by many hundreds, by many thousands, by many myriads, grow up all around. . . . "

Still, the Avesta is a holy book, and it says one type of medicine is preferred. "If several healers offer themselves together . . . namely, one who heals with the knife, one who heals with herbs, and one who heals with the Holy Word, let one apply to the healing by the Holy Word: for this one is the best-healing of all healers who heals with the Holy Word; he will best drive away sickness from the body of the faithful."

Sassanian doctors were expected to pass tests that showed their skills, sometimes using non-Zoroastrians as their test patients. Once they were licensed to practice medicine, many doctors traveled from village to village offering cures. A doctor could be arrested if he refused to treat a sick person who could not afford his services.

In technology, the Sassanians perfected an old device first designed in Greece: the windmill. Either at the end of Sassanian rule or the early years of Muslim rule in Persia, the first practical windmills appeared. The fan blades were made out of fabric. The turning blades and the shaft they were attached to stood up inside a mudbrick building. Wind entered through openings in the building's walls. The earliest windmills appeared in what is now eastern Iran or western Afghanistan and were used to pump water and grind grain.

EPILOGUE

THE ARAB INVASION OF THE 600S ENDED THE LAST OF THE
Persian Empires. A new culture emerged. It combined the conquering
Arab Islamic culture with the many cultural strains that had developed
in Persia since the rise of Cyrus the Great some 1,200 years before. Persia and its former lands would continue to be a meeting place for different cultures for centuries.

LIFE UNDER ARAB RULE

Under the Arabs, Christians and Jews were allowed to practice their
faith, both in Persia and the other lands the Muslims conquered. Followers of those two faiths believed in the same monotheistic God the
Muslims worshipped, and their religion shared roots in the biblical
figure Abraham.

Zoroastrianism was monotheistic, but it did not recognize the Bible
of Jews and Christians. Its division of the universe into good and evil
forces did not blend with Muhammad's teachings, either. Still, the Arabs
decided to let Zoroastrians practice their faith, though historians do not
know how widespread the religion was among the average people.

Over several centuries, many Persians converted to Islam. The upper
classes and merchants were most likely the first to convert. They could
gain influence or money by embracing the religion of their new rulers.

To run the huge lands of the former Persian Empire, the Arabs
needed Sassanian officials to manage the government and, most
importantly, collect taxes. The Sassanian system for controlling
government income and spending was adopted by the Arabs, and

CONNECTIONS

Zoroastrianism Today

The arrival of the Muslim Arabs posed a threat to Zoroastrian Persians. At times, the Muslims burned religious texts and forced the Zoroastrians to convert to Islam, even though the official policy was to tolerate Zoroastrian practice. Through the 10th century, many Zoroastrians left the country and settled in India, where they became known as Parsis. There, many of them became successful business owners, respected for their intelligence and financial skills. Outside of Iran, the largest population following this religion can today be found in Mumbai, India.

Some Zoroastrians remained in Iran. Today, they number about 50,000, and the Iranian government gives them special permission to practice most of their traditional rites.

Since the 1970s, some Iranian Zoroastrians have also settled across the United States. The U.S. Zoroastrian community has about 10,000 members. There is a sizeable Zoroastrian population in Los Angeles. In 2007, a group of young Zoroastrians met at a convention in Chicago. One of them, Neville Vazfidar, said some people see the fires in their temples and think Zoroastrians worship the flames. But as Vazfidar explained to a reporter from the *Chicago Tribune*, "Fire is the symbol of the inner light we strive to realize."

eventually spread to all their lands. In Persia, Sassanian coins also remained in use.

People mostly lived their lives as they had under the Sassanians, with farming and herding dominating the economy. The Persian language also remained in common use, even after Arabic was made the official language of government in 696.

The first Arab dynasty was the Umayyads, who ruled from Damascus, in Syria, starting in 661. Persian influence in the Islamic world grew when the next dynasty, the Abbasids, arose in 750. The Abbasids believed the Umayyads did not rule with popular support, and they overthrew the Umayyads.

The Abbasids set up their capital in Baghdad. Their army had many soldiers from Khorasan, a region of Iran, including a top general, Abu Muslim Khorasani (d. 755). His military efforts helped the Abbasids come to power, and the new dynasty had a good deal of support in Persia. Under their rule, many people moved from the countryside to the cities, where foreign trade helped boost the economy.

These new city dwellers converted to Islam in large numbers. Persians also played a large role in transmitting ideas in math, science, and other subjects.

With the center of the Abbasid government in the heart of former Persian lands, Persian-Sassanian influence remained strong. In politics, one idea that took hold was that the ideal ruler had the blessing of Allah (the Muslim God). Each successive caliph claimed the right to rule because of this blessing. Persian rulers, back to the Achaemenids, had based their right to govern on a similar idea, with Ahura Mazda blessing royal power and rule staying within the dynastic family.

A NEW PERSIAN DYNASTY

Through the ninth century, the Abbasids in Baghdad began to lose some of their central power and control over distant parts of the former Persian Empire. New local dynasties emerged. Power passed from father to son. The caliphs in Baghdad let this local rule develop, since the governors were generally loyal, paid tribute, and kept order. The most famous of these families was the Tahirids, who were based in Khorasan. They claimed to be descended from the Sassanian kings.

Another local dynasty that emerged was the Saffarids, who were centered in Sistan, a region of eastern Iran and southwest Afghanistan. The founder of this dynasty, Yaqub Saffar (840–879), took control of the region from the Tahirids. Saffar even challenged the power of the caliph in Baghdad, but was defeated. Still, his successors continued to control lands in Central Asia. They held onto their power thanks to their loyalty to a new Persian dynasty, the Samanids.

The founder of the Samanid dynasty had four grandsons. The Abbasid rulers gave each of them a province to govern. One of them, Ismail I (d. 907), overthrew the Saffarids and another ruling dynasty in Central Asia. He created an almost-independent Persian state. It included Khorasan, in what is now northeast Iran, and Transoxiana, which included parts of what are now Afghanistan, Uzbekistan, Turkmenistan, Tajikistan, and Kazakhstan.

From their capital in Bukhara, Ismail and his successors ruled for almost 100 years. Eventually, they extended their influence to the borders of India. The Samanids were known for their architecture and support of arts and education. Under their rule, the poet Rudaki (d. 954) began a work called the *Shahnamah* (*The Epic of Kings*). It was finished by a later Persian poet, Firdawsi (ca. 935–ca. 1020).

Shahnamah was based on Arabic translations of writings from the Sassanian era. The original stories told the history of Persia, from mythical kings and heroes through the rule of Khosrow II. Firdawsi spent 30 years finishing this work. The *Shahnamah* is still read and enjoyed in Iran and other Persian-speaking regions.

The poem was the first major work done in a language known today as New Persian, which replaced the Middle Persian of Sassanian times. The new language used Arabic script and adopted some Arabic words. From this time on, Persians used their language for some writing, such as poetry, and used Arabic for religious and legal affairs.

Through the 10th century, the Arab rulers in Baghdad continued to lose power. More local dynasties emerged. To the west of the Samanids were the Buyids. They also were said to have ties to the Sassanians, though later Islamic historians doubted this claim. Their lands were centered around the traditional heart of ancient Persia and Mesopotamia.

The Buyids followed Shiism, a branch of Islam that was not accepted by the caliph and most Muslims. They also honored pre-Islamic Persia by using Middle Persian on a medal and referring to the King of Kings on their coins.

The Buyids also celebrated Navruz, the Persian New Year. Some modern historians, however, say it is wrong to stress the dynasty's link to the past, because the Buyids were as much Islamic as Persian in their overall attitudes.

THE RISE OF THE TURKS

Under Abbasid rule, Turkic-speaking slaves from Central Asia were brought into the caliphate (the lands where the caliph ruled) as warriors. (The Turkic peoples were the ancestors of the residents of such modern countries as Uzbekistan, Kazakhstan, and Kyrgyzstan.) These slaves were known as Mamluks. Through their military skill, some Mamluks were able to take political power in parts of the Abbasid caliphate.

This included Samanid lands. There, in the south, a Mamluk dynasty called the Ghaznavids emerged in the 10th century. They eventually ruled most of eastern Iran, Afghanistan, and parts of what is now Pakistan. Their dynasty lasted until 1186.

The Mamluk Turks were devout Sunni Muslims. Still, they adopted the old Persian forms of government, employed Persian bureaucrats, and promoted Persian culture.

The other Turkic dynasties included the Seljuks and the Qarakhanids. The Seljuks dominated in the lands of the old Persian Empire. Their control stretched from Asia Minor, Syria, Mesopotamia, and Iran, into Transoxiana. That control was not firm for long, though. The Seljuks began their conquests in the mid 11th century, but by the end of the century they were already in decline.

However, they did manage to stay in power in western Iran through most of the 12th century. Other Turkic and Iranian families controlled the rest of their former lands. The Qara Khitai, who came from China, also settled in Muslim lands that had once been part of the Persian Empire.

THE MONGOLS

The arrival of the Qara Khitai was the first sign that new people from the steppe of Central Asia would play a key role in Persian-Iranian history. In 1206, a Mongol leader named Chinggis Khan (1162–1227) united all the Mongol tribes under his rule. Then he began a series of wars that created the largest empire the world had ever seen. He and his warriors conquered lands that had been part of the eastern half of the old Persian Empires.

One of his successors, Hülegü (1217–1265), continued moving west. He captured Baghdad in 1258, ending Arab Muslim rule throughout the region.

The Mongol Empire soon split into four parts, called khanates. Hülegü kept control of what was called the Ilkhanate. This region stretched from the Oxus River to Anatolia, the heart of modern Turkey. His son Abagha (1234–1282) founded his capital in Tabriz, in northwest Iran.

He and Mongols who followed him allowed the Persians, Arabs, and other peoples to practice their own religions, and they relied on

The Mausoleum of Ismail

Bukhara, Uzbekistan, is the site of one of the oldest Muslim mausoleums (an elaborate monument and burial place for the dead) in Central Asia. It was originally built for the father of Ismail, but instead served as the final resting place of later Samanid rulers. The building, a cube with a dome on top, is famous for its dazzling brickwork, set on walls six feet thick. The mausoleum is one of the oldest surviving monuments in Uzbekistan and is an example of Persian-influenced art and building techniques. The mausoleum is so well made that it has supposedly needed almost no repair since it was built more than 1,100 years ago.

Shiites and Sunnis

In the seventh century, a split occurred within Islam, as Muslims disagreed over which of two branches of Muhammad's family had the right to rule as caliph. In what is now Iraq, those who supported Ali (ca. 600– ca. 661)— Muhammad's adopted son—and his descendants created what is called Shiism. This form of Islam has always had fewer followers than the Sunni branch. But in Iran, Shiism won support from the Buyids and other Persian rulers, as well as from the Mongols who invaded Iran in the 13th century. Shiism became the official state religion in Iran in the 16th century. Today Iran has a larger percentage of Shiites (89 percent of the population) than any other nation.

local officials to help them run the government. Persian was widely spoken, and the Mongols came to appreciate the local art and literature. The Mongols, like the ancient Persians before them, also promoted commerce. Shiraz, once famous for its grapes, became a center for iron-making. Markets called bazaars flourished in many cities.

Still, to many Persians living in the Ilkhanate, the Mongol era was a painful time. Hamd Allah Mustawfi (d. ca. 1340) worked for the Mongols. He wrote in the 14th century (as quoted in David Morgan's *The Mongols*), "The destruction which happened on the emergence of the Mongol state and the general massacre that occurred at that time will not be repaired in a thousand years. . . ."

The Ilkhanate ended in 1335. Local rulers held the power until the rise of Timur I (ca. 1336–1405) in the 1370s. Timur was called Tamerlane in Europe. He had Turkic roots but also claimed a family tie to Chinggis Khan. Timur built an empire that included Iran and surrounding lands. But it began to come apart after his death in 1405. His descendants sometimes fought with one another for control of Central Asia. Turkic influence continued to grow in the region.

THE SAFAVID EMPIRE

For a time in the 15th century, Turkic and Persian rulers emerged in parts of Iran. The dynasty that reunited the Persian heartland under a single ruler was the Safavids, founded by Shah Ismail (1487–1524) in 1501. (*Shah* is a Persian word for king.) The Safavids were of Turkic origin and were devout followers of Shiism. Their conquests were part of a holy war against Sunni Muslims. With his victory, Ismail made Shiism the official state religion of Persia. Historians give him and his dynasty credit for creating the political and cultural framework of modern Iran.

Ismail claimed to be descended from many past rulers of Central Asia, including the Sassanians, Alexander the Great, and the legendary kings mentioned in the *Shahnamah*. Like other invaders of Iran, he relied on Persian bureaucrats to run the government. The Persian language was still widely spoken.

After Ismail, one notable Safavid leader was Abbas I (ca. 1557– 1628), who ruled from 1588 to 1628. He made his capital in Isfahan,

south of Tehran, and built impressive mosques (Muslim houses of worship) there that still stand. Abbas also secured Persia's borders and promoted trade and diplomatic contacts with Europe and India. The shah also supported arts. His rule marked the best of Safavid architecture and painting.

After Abbas, the Safavid dynasty lasted almost 100 years. During its last years, starting around 1722, Persia faced invasions by Afghans in the east and Turks in the west. The Afghans controlled some of Persia until 1730, and the Safavid dynasty ended six years later, in 1736.

Through the rest of the 18th century, different tribal leaders took power. Sometimes they backed members of the Safavid family. The most memorable was Nadir Shah (1688–1747), who conquered lands in Transoxiana and India. The Iran Chamber Society Web site calls him "the second Alexander," though his rule never touched as many lands

The Sheikh Lutfallah Mosque was one of the many beautiful mosques built by Safavid leader Abbas I for his new capital in Isfahan.

Tolerant but Insincere

One of the best accounts of life in Safavid Persia comes from Jean Chardin (1643–1713), a well-educated French jeweler who first traveled there in 1665. His book *Travels in Persia* gave Europeans details about the court of the Safavid ruler Suleyman III.

Chardin did not always think highly of his hosts. In a selection from his book, he said the Persians gave many compliments and were skilled at flattery, but they were not sincere.

They understand flattering very well; and though they do it with modesty, yet they do it with art, and insinuation [suggestions]. You would say, that they intend as they speak, and would swear to it: Nevertheless, as soon as the occasion is over, such as a prospect of interest, or a regard of compliance, you plainly see that all their compliments were very far from being sincere.

He also felt the Persians lied and cheated. Yet Chardin also found many positives. (Clergy are religious officials, such as priests.)

The most commendable property of the manners of the Persians, is their kindness to strangers; the reception and protection they afford them, and their universal hospitality, and toleration, in regard to religion, except the clergy of the country, who, as in all other places, hate to a furious degree, all those that differ from their opinions. The Persians are very civil, and very honest in matters of religion . . . They believe that all men's prayers are good and prevalent; therefore, in their illnesses, and in other wants, they admit of, and even desire the prayers of different religions: I have seen it practiced a thousand times.

(Source: Chardin, Jean. "Persians: Kind, Hospitable, Tolerant, Flattering Cheats?" Iranian.com. Available online. URL: http://www.iranian.com/Travelers/June97/Chardin/index.shtml. Accessed May 8, 2008.)

as Alexander the Great's. But, like Alexander, Nadir Shah did not rule long, and he failed to build a lasting dynasty.

Another Safavid then sat on the throne (Ismail III), but the real power was with Karim Khan Zand (ca. 1705–1779), a general under Nadir Shah. Zand let the British build a trading post in Iran. He died in 1779, and various members of his family struggled for power. That struggle ended with the emergence of a new tribal dynasty, the Qajars.

THE QAJARS AND THE PAHLAVIS

Coming from Azerbaijan in northwest Persia, the Qajars took control in 1796. The dynasty founder, Agha Muhammad Shah (1720–1797), reunited Persia and moved the capital to Tehran, where it remains today. During Qajar rule, the Russians and British influenced Persian politics, as those two European powers competed for dominance in Central Asia. The borders of Persia shrunk and the central government lost power, though modern technology, such as the telegraph and railroad, entered the country.

As Russian and British influence kept increasing in the region, a Persian political activist named Jamal al-Din al-Afghani (1838–1897) called for a return to traditional culture. He also saw the need for a more efficient government, but he said the Persians could improve their lives without Western help. He and others wanted a government based on a constitution, rather than religious rule or a kingship. A constitution finally came in 1906–1907, creating a government with elected lawmakers. The shah became more like a modern president than the traditional King of Kings.

The new government, however, did not run smoothly. Persia faced several years of disorder. World War I (1914–1918) added to the troubles, as Turkish, Russian, and British troops all occupied parts of Persia. When the war ended, Great Britain tried once again to assert strong control over Persia. A wave of nationalism (strong support for one's own country and its independence from foreign influences) spread over the people. They wanted a Persian government, and one strong enough to effectively run the country. That government came in 1921, as some nationalists and an army force known as the Cossacks ended the Qajar dynasty.

Birth of the Bahai Faith

Under the Qajars, a new religion emerged in Persia. It had its roots in the teachings of a Shiite Persian who was known as the Bab (1819–1850). He called for greater rights for women and the poor. One of his followers, Bahaullah (1817–1892), claimed in 1852 that he was a prophet and had received a vision of from God. Bahaullah then gathered his own followers, creating what is known as the Bahai Faith.

Bahaullah said God wanted humans to live in full equality. Each person had to find their faith on their own, not through priests. God created humans, he said (as quoted at Baha'i.org), so "that they may work for the betterment of the world and live together in concord and harmony."

Bahaullah's views angered the government and Muslim religious authorities, and he was forced to leave Persia. His teachings, though, continued to spread. Today, the Bahai Faith has its headquarters in Haifa, Israel, and claims about 5 million members around the world.

One of the leaders of this government takeover was Reza Khan (1877–1944). Within five years, he became the founder of a new Persian dynasty, called the Pahlavi. The name came from the founders of the old Parthian empire. Reza Khan would sometimes look back to Persia's past while also trying to make it a modern nation.

Under Reza Khan, Persia had its first permanent professional army since the days of the Achaemenids. He also officially changed Persia's name to Iran, creating a link to the Aryans who had settled the region thousands of years before. Although Iran had a constitution and Reza Khan was elected to the position of shah, he ruled more like the kings of old, doing what he thought was best for the nation.

The Pahlavi dynasty changed Persia's name to Iran in 1935. Today the country plays a major role in global politics.

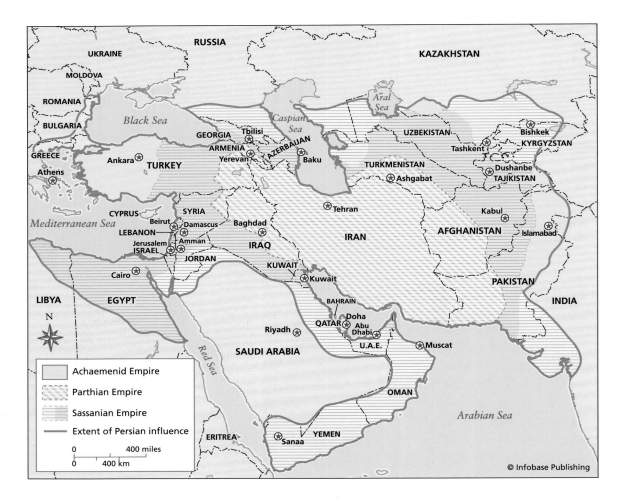

© Infobase Publishing

World War II (1939–1945) brought more foreign occupation and an end to Reza Khan's rule. He stepped down in 1941 and his son Muhammad Reza (1919–1980) took over as shah. However, the British, Russians, and Americans actually controlled the country throughout the war. By this time, Iran was known to have vast reserves of oil. This would become an important source of wealth in the years to come.

After the war, Muhammad Reza tried to assert his power. He strengthened the military, which he directly controlled, and limited public criticism of his rule. Opposing him were nationalists, led by Muhammad Mosaddeq (1880–1967). In 1951, Mosaddeq became prime minister. The two men struggled for control. The U.S. and British governments opposed Mosaddeq's policies—which included taking control of the oil industry which was at the time in British hands. The Americans secretly aided street mobs that forced Mosaddeq out of the government in 1953. From then on, Muhammad Reza ruled with strong U.S. support. But he limited freedoms and made many enemies.

REVOLUTIONARY IRAN

Muhammad Reza's policies angered Iranian nationalists and people who wanted democracy. He also angered Shiite religious leaders, who wanted a return to strict Muslim rule. These different groups united against Muhammad Reza. In January 1979, after many protests against his rule, the shah left the country.

Soon, a Shiite religious leader named Ayatollah Ruhollah Khomeini (ca. 1900–1989) was in control of the government. Later that year, some of his followers kidnapped more than 50 Americans working in Tehran. They were held hostage for more than one year, creating a split in U.S.-Iranian relations that remains today.

Under Khomeini and the Shiite leaders, Iran became a

CONNECTIONS

Persian Words in English

Bazaar, the name for a market selling a variety of goods, is just one of many words with Persian roots that is used in English. Many of the most common words relate to food. They include *candy, lemon, sherbet, orange,* and *julep* (a type of sweet cocktail). Other words with Persian roots are *jackal* (a fox-like animal), *pajama, turban* (a type of headgear), and *scarlet* (deep red).

The modern descendants of the ancient Persians, such as these women in Iran, bridge the gap between the old empire and the modern world.

strict Islamic state. Laws were based on the Quran, the Islamic holy book. The rights of women were limited. The religious leaders tried to keep out Western influences, although modern technology—cell phones, satellite television, the Internet—made that difficult. They did not identify with the great Persian past, as Muhammad Reza and his father had. They also used their wealth from oil to fund terrorist groups opposed to Israel and the Western world.

To some U.S. leaders, Iran is a growing threat. Iran is currently developing nuclear facilities that it says are for peaceful purposes. But its seeming desire for nuclear weapons fuels fears around the world.

The recent bad relations between Iran and the United States makes many Americans suspicious of Iran and its intentions. The troubles may also keep people from understanding Iran's past. The Iranian people, however, know that they have deep roots and that the ancient Persians made important contributions to world culture.

The Achaemenids, Parthians, and Sassanians served as links between different regions of the world. Many of the Persian kings supported art and science that are still valued today. And the Persians, according to Yale law professor Amy Chua in her 2007 book *Day of Empire*, built the first "hyperpower." Achaemenid Persia, like other super-powerful states, Chua believes, "was, at least by the standards of its time, extraordinarily pluralistic and tolerant during its rise. . . ." The Persian Empires are worthy of study today because of their great accomplishments, and because their descendants play a crucial role in world affairs.

Time Line

ca. 559 B.C.E.	Cyrus the Great takes power in Persia, beginning the Achaemenid dynasty.
550 B.C.E.	Cyrus defeats the Medes, uniting them and the Persians under his rule.
539 B.C.E.	Persia conquers Babylonia.
525 B.C.E.	Cambyses II defeats Egypt and it becomes part of the Persian Empire.
ca. 522 B.C.E.	Darius the Great takes the throne and begins to expand the empire.
490 B.C.E.	Persia invades Greece and is defeated at Marathon.
480 B.C.E.	The Greeks hold off a second Persian invasion.
401 B.C.E.	Civil war between Artaxerxes II and Cyrus the Younger ends with Cyrus's defeat.
330 B.C.E.	Alexander the Great of Macedon defeats Darius and takes control of the Persian Empire, ending the Achaemenid dynasty.
323 B.C.E.	Alexander the Great dies. His empire begins to split into separate kingdoms that are under Greek rule.
247 B.C.E.	The Arsacid dynasty is founded in Parthia, marking the rise of a new Persian Empire.
171 B.C.E.	Mithridates I takes power in Parthia and begins the expansion of Parthian Persia.
53 B.C.E.	The first of several wars is fought between Parthia and the Roman Empire.
217 C.E.	The Parthians have their last major victory over Rome, at Nisibis (in what is now southeastern Turkey).
224	Ardashir defeats the Parthian king in battle, marking the emergence of the Sassanian dynasty and the end of the Arsacid dynasty.
233	The Sassanians prevent the Romans from taking Ctesiphon. This marks the end of the first of several wars between the two empires.
298	A peace treaty forces the Persians to give back land they had previously taken from Rome.
531	The reign of Khosrow I, the last great Sassanian king, begins.
637	Arab Muslims conquer the Persian capital of Ctesiphon.
651	The death of Yazdagird III marks the complete victory of the Arabs and the end of the Sassanian dynasty and the last Persian Empire.

GLOSSARY

allies people who work together, especially to fight a common enemy

archaeologist a scientist who studies ancient peoples by studying the items they left behind

archer someone skilled in the use of a bow and arrow

architecture the way buildings are designed and built; the people who design and build them are *architects*

aristocracy a small group of people believed to be the best members of society, or who have the most money and power

artisan a person skilled in a certain craft, such as making pottery or working with metal

booty wealth taken from the losing side after a victory in battle

bureaucracy professional officials who carry out the daily operations of a government

catapult a large machine used to hurl heavy objects

cavalry soldiers who fight on horseback

city-state an independent political unit consisting of a city and the surrounding countryside that comes under its rule

civil relating to the general public and its affairs, separate from military or religious affairs

civilizations great nations or peoples and their ways of living, including their art, religion, education, and society.

cleric a religious official

commerce the activity of buying and selling

concubine a woman who is supported by a man and lives with him without being legally married to him

constitution a document that outlines a nation's government and its basic laws

descendants relatives who trace their roots back to one person

domesticated animals animals bred for use in agriculture

dynasty a family that keeps control of a government over many generations, with rule often passed from a parent to a child

elites the wealthy, powerful classes in a society

fertility the ability to produce crops (for land) or offspring (for animals and people)

Hellenized adopted the language and culture of the Greeks; the adjective is *Hellenic*

hoplite a heavily armed Greek foot soldier

infantry soldiers who fight on foot

inscription writing, usually carved into stone or metal, that is meant to leave a lasting record of events

jousting fighting on horseback between two riders equipped with lances

lance a long, pointed weapon often used by soldiers on horseback

mercenary a professional soldier who will fight for any army that pays him

Mesopotamia ancient name for the region between the Tigris and Euphrates Rivers, in what is now Iraq

monotheism worshipping only one god; the adjective is monotheistic

moral choosing to act correctly

nationalism strong support for one's own country and its independence from foreign influences; people who feel this way are nationalists

nobility   the upper class of society

nomad   a person with no permanent home who wanders from place to place

oasis   an area with water in the middle of a desert

peninsula   an area of land surrounded by water on three sides

persecute   attack or deny the legal rights of a particular group

plateau   a raised area of land that is flat on top

prophet   a person who claims to speak for a god

province   a region within a country, often with its own local ruler

qanat   an underground canal that carries water over long distances

rations   food and drink given out over a specific time period, such daily or weekly

reign   the length of time a particular ruler is in power

relief   sculpture created by carving away the surrounding rock or other material to leave an image that rises off the background

rhyton   a fancy, cone-shaped drinking cup

rites   solemn or important religious acts or ceremonies

satrap   a regional Persian governor; the area he controls is a satrapy

scribe   someone whose job is to write down all important records

siege   cutting off a town or fort from the outside so it cannot receive supplies and citizens cannot escape

stucco   fine plaster used to coat the outside of walls and to mold into decorations on buildings

successor   the ruler who comes after the current ruler; the line of successors is the succession

temple   a building where religious ceremonies are held

textiles   cloth and items made from cloth

treasury   the part of a government that collects taxes and pays bills; also, the place where this money is stored

tribute   money or goods paid to a foreign ruler to prevent an invasion or show obedience

Western   the parts of the world, particularly Europe and the United States, that were heavily influenced by Greek and Roman culture and tend to have democratic governments

BIBLIOGRAPHY

"Achaemenid Soil Dam Discovered in Fars Province." Cultural Heritage News Agency, March 12, 2007. Available online. URL: http://www.chnpress. com/news/?section=2&id=7033. Accessed April 21, 2008.

Allen, Lindsay, *The Persian Empire*. Chicago: University of Chicago Press, 2005.

Arrian, "The Anabasis of Alexander." Iran Chamber Society. Available online. URL: http://www.iran chamber.com/history/achaemenids/arrian_battle_ of_gaugamela.php. Accessed February 5, 2008.

"Avesta–Zoroastrian Archives." Available online. URL: http://www.avesta.org/avesta.html. Accessed May 1, 2008.

"The Bahai Faith." Available online. URL: http://www. bahai.org/. Accessed May 3, 2008.

"The Behistun inscription." Livius: Articles on Ancient History. Available online. URL: http:// www.livius.org/be-bm/behistun/behistun03.html. Accessed February 12, 2008.

Briant, Pierre, *From Cyrus to Alexander: A History of the Persian Empire*. Translated by Peter T. Daniels. Winona Lake, Ind.: Eisenbrauns, 2002.

Brosius, Maria, *The Persians: An Introduction.* New York: Routledge, 2006.

———, *Women in Ancient Persia, 559-331 B.C.* Oxford, U.K.: Clarendon Press, 1996.

"Canadian Zurkhaneh Sports Federation." Available online. URL: http://www.zurkhaneh.ca. Accessed March 1, 2008.

"The Canal of Xerxes in Northern Greece: Explorations 1991–2001." Institute of Geodynamics, National Observatory of Athens. Available online. URL: http://www.gein.noa.gr/xerxes_canal/ ENG_XERX/ENGWEB.htm. Accessed February 18, 2008.

Cantor, Norman, editor, *The Encyclopedia of the Middle Ages*. New York: Viking Press, 1999.

Cartledge, Paul, *Alexander the Great: The Hunt for a New Past.* Woodstock, N.Y.: The Overlook Press, 2004.

Cassius Dio, *Roman History*. Lacus Curtius. Available online. URL: http://penelope.uchicago.edu/Thayer/ E/Roman/Texts/Cassius_Dio/home.html. Accessed February 12, 2008.

Chardin, Jean, "Persians: Kind, Hospitable, Tolerant, Flattering Cheats?" Iranian.com. Available online. URL: http://www.iranian.com/Travelers/June97/ Chardin/index.shtml. Accessed May 8, 2008.

"Chronicle of Nabonidus." Livius: Articles on Ancient History. Available online. URL: http://www.livius. org/ct-cz/cyrus_I/babylon02.html#Chronicle%20of %20Nabonidus. Accessed March 4, 2008.

Chua, Amy, *Day of Empire: How Hyperpowers Rise to Global Dominance—and Why They Fall*. New York: Doubleday, 2007.

"Circle of Ancient Iranian Studies." Available online. URL: http://www.cais-soas.com/CAIS/frontpage. htm. Accessed February 1, 2008.

Curtis, John, editor, *Mesopotamia and Iran in the Parthian and Sasanian Periods: Rejection and Revival, c. 238 B.C.–A.D. 642*. London: British Museum Press, 2000.

"Cyrus Cylinder (2)," Livius: Articles on Ancient History. Available online. URL: http://www.livius. org/ct-cz/cyrus_I/cyrus_cylinder2.html. Accessed February 15, 2008.

Dahl, Fredrik, "In Iran, Ancient Rite Links God and Wrestling." *Daily Times*, September 6, 2007. Available online. URL: http://www.dailytimes.com.pk/ default.asp?page=2007%5C09%5C06%5Cstory_6-9- 2007_pg4_21. Accessed March 1, 2008.

Dareini, Ali Akbar, "Iran Dam Said to Threaten Ancient Sites." *Washington Post*, April 19, 2007. Available online. URL: http://www.washington-post.com/wp-dyn/content/article/2007/04/19/AR2007041901942.html. Accessed February 11, 2008.

"Darius' building inscription from Susa." Livius: Articles on Ancient History. Available online. URL: http://www.livius.org/da-dd/darius/darius_i_t03.html. Accessed June 25, 2008.

De Souza, Philip, *The Greek and Persian Wars 499–386 B.C.* New York: Routledge, 2003.

Dignas, Beate, and Engelbert Winter, *Rome and Persia in Late Antiquity: Neighbours and Rivals.* Cambridge, U.K.: Cambridge University Press, 2007.

Diodorus of Sicily, *Library.* Perseus Digital Library. Available online. URL: http://www.perseus.tufts.edu/cgi-bin/ptext?layout=;doc=Perseus%3Atext%3A1999.01.0084;query=toc;loc=9.1.1. Accessed March 1, 2008.

"Encyclopedia Iranica." Available online. URL: http://www.iranica.com/newsite/aboutiranica/index.isc. Accessed February 4, 2008.

"Fall of Nineveh Chronicle." Livius: Articles on Ancient History. Available online. URL: http://www.livius.org/ne-nn/nineveh/nineveh02.html. Accessed March 3, 2008.

Farrokh, Kaveh, *Shadows in the Desert: Ancient Persia at War.* Oxford, U.K.: Osprey Publishing, 2007.

"Forgotten Empire: The World of Ancient Persia." Available online. URL: http://thebritishmuseum.ac.uk/forgottenempire/palaces/index.html. Accessed February 3. 2008.

Frood, Arran, "Riddle of 'Baghdad's Batteries.'" BBC News, February 27, 2003. Available online. URL: http://news.bbc.co.uk/2/hi/science/nature/2804257.stm. Accessed May 1, 2008.

Garthwaite, Gene R., *The Persians.* Oxford, U.K.: Blackwell Publishing, 2005.

Gershevitch, Ilya, editor, *The Cambridge History of Iran: Vol. 2, The Median and Achaemenian Periods.* Cambridge, U.K.: Cambridge University Press, 1985.

Ghavidel, Hedieh, "The History of Medicine in Ancient Persia." Press TV, January 28, 2008. Available online. URL: http://www.presstv.ir/detail.aspx?id=40689&sectionid=3510304. Accessed March 25. 2008.

Goetzmann, William, "Financing Civilization." Yale School of Management. Available online. URL: http://viking.som.yale.edu/will/finciv/chapter1.htm. Accessed April 22, 2008.

Grossman, Ron, "Keeping Their Faith's Flame Lit." *Chicago Tribune*, October 15, 2007.

Hadjialiloo, Arash, "Federal Court Threatens Iranian-American Heritage." National Iranian American Council, March 12, 2008. Available online. URL: http://www.niacouncil.org/index.php?Itemid=2&id=1059&option=com_content&task=view. Accessed April 21, 2008.

Haney, William P., "Mithridates and Mithridatum." *San Diego Physician*, December 2004. Available online. URL: http://www.sdcms.org/atf/cf/%7B2246CA5C-0E62-45D2-B736-9A9D35AFFAF9%7D/2004.12.SDP.haney.pdf. Accessed February 17, 2008.

Harrison, Frances, "Iran's Proud But Discreet Jews." BBC News, September 22, 2006. Available online. URL: http://news.bbc.co.uk/2/hi/middle_east/5367892.stm. Accessed April 28, 2008.

Herodian, *History of the Roman Empire since the Death of Marcus Aurelius.* Livius: Articles on Ancient History. Available online. URL: http://www.livius.org/he-hg/herodian/hre000.html. Accessed June 30, 2008.

Herodotus, *The History.* Translated by David Greene. Chicago: University of Chicago Press, 1987.

———, *The Histories.* Translated by Robin Waterfield. Oxford, U.K.: Oxford University Press, 1998.

Holland, Tom, *Persian Fire: The First World Empire and the Battle for the West.* New York: Anchor Books, 2007.

Hourani, Albert, *A History of the Arab Peoples.* Cambridge, Mass.: Belknap Press, 1991.

Houseman, Mordecai, translator, *The Book of Esther.* "Purim Gateway." Being Jewish. Available online. URL: http://www.beingjewish.com/yomtov/purim/esther_intro.html. Accessed March 3, 2008.

Ikram, Salima, "Cambyses' Lost Army." *Archaeology*, Volume 3, Number 5 (September/October 2000).

Available online. URL: http://www.archaeology. org/0009/newsbriefs/cambyses.html. Accessed February 12, 2008.

"The Inscription of Shapur I at Naqsh-e-Rustam in Fars." Translated by R. N. Frye. *The History of Ancient Iran*. Available online. URL: http://www. colorado.edu/classics/clas4091/Text/Shapur.htm. Accessed April 29, 2008.

"Iran's Oldest Game." *Persian Journal*, December 4, 2004. Available online. URL: http://www.iranian. ws/iran_news/publish/article_20127.shtml. Accessed May 1. 2008.

"Iranian Three-Story Underground City Served as Haven." Payvand's Iran News, August 2, 2004. Available online. URL: http://www.payvand. com/news/04/aug/1013.html. Accessed April 24, 2008.

Irving, Mark, "Muscular Shias Return to Roots." BBC News, April 22, 2004. Available online. URL: http:// news.bbc.co.uk/2/hi/middle_east/3647621.stm. Accessed May 1. 2008.

James, Peter, and Nick Thorpe, *Ancient Invention*. New York: Ballantine Books, 1994.

Josephus, Flavius, *The Antiquities of the Jews*. The Works of Flavius Josephus. Available online. URL: http://www.ccel.org/j/josephus/works/JOSEPHUS. HTM. Accessed February 10, 2008.

Justinus, Marcus Junianus, *Epitome of the Philippic History of Pompeius Trogus*. Corpus Scriptorum Latinorum. Available online. URL: http://www. forumromanum.org/literature/justin/english/ index.html. Accessed February 18, 2008.

"Letter from Artabanus II to Susa." Parthia.com. Available online. URL: http://www.parthia.com/ artabanus2_letter.htm. Accessed July 2, 2008.

Lewis, D. M., et al., editors, *The Cambridge Ancient History: Vol. 6, The Fourth Century B.C.* Cambridge, U.K.: Cambridge University Press, 1994.

Litvinsky, B. A., editor, *History of the Civilizations of Central Asia: Vol. 3, The Crossroads of Civilizations, A.D. 250–750*. Paris: UNESCO, 1996.

McEvedy, Colin, *The New Penguin Atlas of Ancient History*, 2nd ed. London: Penguin Books, 2002.

Merriam-Webster's Biographical Dictionary. Springfield, Mass.: Merriam-Webster, 1995.

Merriam-Webster's Collegiate Dictionary, 10th ed. Springfield, Mass.: Merriam Webster, 1997.

Merriam-Webster's Geographical Dictionary, 3rd ed. Springfield, Mass.: Merriam Webster, 1997.

"Mesopotamian chronicles." Livius: Articles on Ancient History. Available online. URL: http:// www.livius.org/cg-cm/chronicles/chron00.html. Accessed June 1, 2008.

Morgan, David, *The Mongols*, 2nd ed. Oxford, U.K.: Blackwell Publishers, 2007.

O'Brien, Patrick K., general editor, *Oxford Atlas of World History*. New York: Oxford University Press, 1999.

"The Parthian Empire." Available online. URL: http:// www.parthia.com/. Accessed March 5, 2008.

"Persepolis fortification tablets." Livius: Articles on Ancient History. Available online. URL: http:// www.livius.org/pen-pg/persepolis/fortification_ tablets.html. Accessed February 18, 2008.

"Persian Carpets: A Brief History." IranSaga. Available online. URL: http://www.art-arena.com/pcarpet. htm. Accessed April 28, 2008.

"The Persian Carpet Gallery." Iranian Cultural & Information Center. Available online. URL: http:// www.persia.org/Images/Persian_Carpet/carpet_ history.html. Accessed April 28, 2008.

Peterson, Scott, "In Ahmadinejad's Iran, Jews Still Find a Space." *Christian Science Monitor*, April 27, 2007. Available online. URL: http://www.csmonitor. com/2007/0427/p01s03-wome.html. Accessed April 28, 2008.

Plutarch, *Lives*. The Internet Classics Archives. Available online. URL: http://classics.mit.edu/ Browse/index-Plutarch.html. Accessed February 12, 2008.

———. *Lives*. Lacus Curtius. Available online. URL: http://penelope.uchicago.edu/Thayer/E/Roman/ Texts/Plutarch/Lives/home.html. Accessed March 2, 2008.

Records of Ardashir. Ancient History Sourcebook. Available online. URL: http://www.fordham.edu/ halsall/ancient/ardashir.html. Accessed March 30, 2008.

"Roads of Time Converge in Bolaghi Valley." Mehr News, September 10, 2007. Available online.

URL: http://www.mehrnews.ir/en/NewsDetail. aspx?NewsID=549887. Accessed February 11, 2008.

"Skunkha." Livius: Articles on Ancient History. Available online. URL: http://www.livius.org/sj-sn/skunkha/skunkha.html. Accessed June 1, 2008.

"The story of Wedjahor-Resne." Livius: Articles on Ancient History. Available online. URL: http://www.livius.org/w/wedjahorresne/wedjahorresne.htm. Accessed June 24, 2008.

Stronk, Jan P., "Pierre Briant, Darius dans l'ombre d'Alexandre," *Bryn Mawr Classical Review,* March 10, 2004. Available online. URL: http://ccat.sas.upenn.edu/bmcr/2004/2004-03-10.html. Accessed February 14, 2008.

Tacitus, *The Annals.* The Internet Classics Archives. Available online. URL: http://classics.mit.edu/Tacitus/annals.html. Accessed March 12, 2008.

Thucydides, *History of the Peloponnesian War.* Translated by Rex Warner. New York: Penguin Books, 1973.

"UNEP Calls for Action Plan to Save Iraqi Marshlands." Global Security.org, March 24, 2003. Available online. URL: http://www.globalsecurity.org/wmd/library/news/iraq/2003/iraq-030324-usia09.htm. Accessed February 4, 2008.

"UNESCO World Heritage Center." Available online. URL: http://whc.unesco.org/. Accessed February 2. 2008.

Van Gelder, G. J. H., *Close Relationships: Incest and Inbreeding in Classic Arabian Literature.* London: I. B. Tauris, 2005.

Wiesehofer, Josef, *Ancient Persia: From 550 B.C. to 650 A.D.*, New edition. London: I.B. Tauris, 2007.

"Wit and Wine: A New Look at Ancient Iranian Ceramics." Teachers' Guide, McClung Museum. Available online. URL: http://mcclungmuseum.utk.edu/specex/witwine/teachersguide.pdf. Accessed February 10, 2008.

Wood, Michael, *In the Footsteps of Alexander the Great.* Berkeley, Calif.: University of California Press, 1997.

Xenophon, *The Education of Cyrus.* Translated by Wayne Ambler. Ithaca, N.Y.: Cornell University Press, 2001.

———. *The Expedition of Cyrus.* Translated by Robin Waterfield. Oxford, U.K.: Oxford University Press, 2005.

Yarshater, Ehsan, editor, *The Cambridge History of Iran: Vol. 3(I), The Seleucid, Parthian, and Sasanian Periods.* Cambridge, U.K.: Cambridge University Press, 1983.

"Yasna 12—The Zoroastrian Creed," Translated by Joseph H. Peterson. Avesta–Zoroastrian Archives. Available online. URL: http://www.avesta.org/yasna/y12j.htm. Accessed May 3. 2008.

FURTHER RESOURCES

BOOKS

Allen, Lindsay, *The Persian Empire* (Chicago: University of Chicago Press, 2005)

> This book focuses on the Achaemenids—their rise to power in Pearsis and Media, the conquests of Cyrus and Darius, and the rule of the kings who followed them. It is filled with beautiful color pictures. The book also traces some of the history of the archaeological work done in Iran, Mesopotamia, and surrounding areas.

Bancroft-Hunt, Norman, *Historical Atlas of Ancient Mesopotamia* (New York: Checkmark Books, 2004)

> More than a collection of maps, this atlas provides details on the lives of the various people who lived and ruled in Mesopotamia, the birthplace of farming, the alphabet, and other key aspects of civilization. The great kingdoms before the Persian Empire—including Sumer, Akkadia, Assyria, and Babylonia—are all featured. For the Persians, the author looks at all three great dynasties, ending with the fall of the Sassanian Empire to the Arabs. Through 40 full-color maps, pictures, and text, the book highlights Persia's conflict with others and daily life in Persian Mesopotamia.

Barter, James, *The Ancient Persians* (Farmington Hills, Mich.: Lucent Books, 2006)

> This is a look at the Achaemenids. The book starts the history of Persia thousands of years before their rise to power. One chapter focuses on the "war machine" of the Persians, their military strategy and tactics both on land and at sea. The book ends with Darius III's loss of the empire to Alexander the Great in 333 B.C.E.

Batmanglij, Najmieh, *Happy Navruz: Cooking with Children to Celebrate the Persian New Year* (Washington, D.C.: Mage Publishers, 2008)

> This illustrated book combines information about the history and customs of Navruz, the Persian New Year, with 25 tasty recipes for Norwuz feasts. The featured dishes range from flatbreads to fish strips to Popsicle desserts. Step-by-step photos make the cooking easy. There are also Navruz activities, such as decorating eggs.

Brosius, Maria, *The Persians: An Introduction* (New York: Routledge, 2006)

> This book gives an overview of the three Persian empires that existed between 550 B.C.E. and 642 C.E. It is written by a well-known scholar of Persian history. For each period, Brosius gives a historical overview, then offers greater details about life at the royal court, art, architecture, and religion. The author is known for her studies of Persian women, and she also offers a closer look at their life during the empires.

Gray, Leon, *Iran* (Washington, D.C.: National Geographic, 2008)

> This book offers an overview of modern Iran, including its roots in ancient Persia from a publisher famous for its striking color photos and great detail. It includes a look at the country's geography, the influence of Islam after the Persians, and the country's current affairs.

Hartz, Paula R., *Zoroastrianism* (New York: Chelsea House, 2009)

> In ancient times, Zoroastrianism was one of major religions of the Near East. This book traces the life of Zoroaster and his founding of the religion that bears his name. It discusses the religion's history, scripture, philosophy, ethics, and rituals. Zoroastrianism is said to have influenced other faiths, such as Judaism and Christianity.

Khonari, Mehdi, M. R. Moghtader, and Minouch Yavari, *The Persian Garden: Echoes of Paradise* (Washington, D.C.: Mage Publishers, 2004)

> For more than 3,000 years, the Persian garden has influenced the art, literature, and even religion of Persia. This book follows the history of the Persian garden and explains the philosophy behind Persian garden design. The book was created by a photographer and architect, Reza Moghtader. Beautiful illustrations and photos take one from the magnificent sanctuaries and hunting parks of fifth-century B.C.E. Persepolis to the enchanting gardens of 19th-century Tehran. There are also photos of garden-carpets, textiles, miniature paintings, stone reliefs, painted tiles, and pottery.

Skelton, Debra, and Pamela Dell, *Empire of Alexander the Great* (New York: Chelsea House, 2009)

> This book looks at the rise of Macedon and Alexander the Great. Alexander conquered all of Greece before heading to Asia and defeating the vast Achaemenid Empire of the Persians. Then, the generals who followed him brought a layer of Greek culture to the Persian heartland and surrounding regions. The Greeks learned from the Persians as well.

Xenophon, *The Expedition of Cyrus*, Translated by Robert Waterfield (New York: Oxford University Press, 2005)

> This new translation of Xenophon's *Anabasis* gives a modern feel to one of the greatest adventure stories of the ancient world. Xenophon, a Greek general serving a Persian prince, described the march of thousands of Greek soldiers across much of the eastern half of the first Persian Empire. His book shows the lives of those soldiers under difficult conditions and offers a Greek view of Persian culture under the Achaemenid dynasty.

DVDS

Persepolis: Rediscovering the Lost Capital of the Persian Empire (Kultur Video, 2009)

> In this DVD, two modern architects use computer animation to reconstruct Persepolis before Alexander the Great's army destroyed it. This documentary film also explores the history and culture of the Persian people of that era.

The Persians: Engineering an Empire (The History Channel, 2006)

> This DVD looks at the engineering achievements of the Achaemenid dynasty. These include a new system of water management, a paved roadway 1,500 miles long, and a canal linking the Nile River to the Red Sea. Interviews with historians and other experts are combined with scenes of modern-day ruins and computer-animated recreations.

WEB SITES

Achaemenid Persia

http://members.ozemail.com.au/~ancientpersia/index.html

> This site contains information about ancient Persia during the Achaemenid dynasty. The site has articles about history and timelines, but also takes a detailed look at Persian culture and everyday life. Fun pages include trivia, quizzes, and games.

Ancient West Asia

www.historyforkids.org/learn/westasia/index.htm

> All the peoples of ancient West Asia are discussed on this site, including the Persians, Assyrians, Mesopotamians, Babylonians, and others. The section on Persia includes a basic

history. A time line and sections in art, culture, language, religion, clothing, science, and more cover the entire region. Also available is information about Alexander the Great.

Forgotten Empire: The World of Ancient Persia
www.thebritishmuseum.ac.uk/forgottenempire/palaces/index.html

This Web site from the British Museum features examples of art and architecture from the Achaemenid dynasty, modern depictions of what historians think Persepolis was like, and a history of the empire and its greatest kings. The site also provides a look over time at the efforts to uncover and understand the treasures of Persepolis.

Iran Chamber Society
www.iranchamber.com/index.php

One of the most comprehensive sites on the Internet for information about Iran, past and present. The section on art and culture looks at monuments from the past, describes the religions in Iran, offers recipes for Persian food, and gives examples of Persian art both modern and ancient. The section on history has articles from the days of the Elamites through the revolution of 1979. Famous Persians/Iranians from the 7th century to today are also profiled.

Livius: Articles on Ancient History—Persia
www.livius.org/persia.html

Part of a larger site devoted to ancient history, this section on Persia explores the history of the Achaemenids, with some information on the Parthians and Sassanians as well. The site provides translation of the Cyrus Cylinder and the Behistun inscriptions. Where appropriate, links take the reader to articles on Greek, Roman, and other ancient peoples who interacted with the Persians.

Musee Achémenide
www.museum-achemenet.college-de-france.fr/

This French site features the work of Pierre Brant, one of the world's experts on Achaemenid Persia. A series of short films, translated into English, use images, narration, and maps to trace the history of Cyrus and his successors. Other images include art objects and illustrations of Persian sites.

Parthia.com
www.parthia.com/

This site focuses on the history of Parthia through its coins, and it also has an overview of the empire's history, geography, art, and culture. Links provide examples of some of the art. The site also has yearly updates, starting in 2000, on excavations under way at Nisa, one of the Parthian capitals.

Persepolis 3D
www.persepolis3d.com

Using digital technology, an Iranian and a German architect are creating three-dimensional images of how Persepolis looked almost 2,500 years ago. The project is ongoing, and samples of what are available to date can be seen at the Web site. They include images of the entire Persepolis building complex and more detailed pictures of the individual buildings, their columns, and the artwork inside.

Sasanika
www.humanities.uci.edu/sasanika/index.html

This resource from the University of California at Irvine is one of the few Web sites on the Internet devoted to the Sassanians. There are links to several Sassanian texts and texts about the Sassanians from ancient writers, as well as examples of recent research. The image gallery has recent pictures of sites and inscriptions that date to the Sassanians.

PICTURE CREDITS

INDEX

About the Author

Michael Burgan has written more than 200 books including *Buddhist Faith in America* (for Facts On File), *Cold War*, and *Colonial and Revolutionary Times*. He has also written biographies of former secretary of state Madeleine Albright, astronaut John Glenn, various U.S. presidents, and several scientists and explorers.

Historical consultant **Thomas G. Urban** received his Masters Degree in Northwest Semitics from the University of Chicago in 2000. He has been senior editor of serial publications in the Publications Office at the Oriental Institute of the University of Chicago since 1990. The Oriental Institute is a world renown publisher of books on the Near East, from Libya to Iran.